Maximum
Strength

Maximum
Strength

Addiction Recovery for
Addicts that Regularly Relapse

by Ross Remien

Silver Torch Press

Beverly Hills, CA

Maximum Strength: Addiction Recovery for Addicts that Regularly Relapse © 2018 by Ross Remien

rossremien.com
rossremien@gmail.com

Printed in the United States of America.

ISBN: 978-1-942707-75-2
Library of Congress Control Number: 2018931892

 Published by Silver Torch Press
www.SilverTorchPress.com
Jill@SilverTorchPress.com

Dedication

I'd like to dedicate this book to my family.

Thanks for putting up with me for all those years.
My actions took a toll on each of you differently.
I'm so sorry for the pain and worry I caused each of you.

Please accept my heartfelt apologies.

Acknowledgements

I first would like to thank Will Vought. Will, you started this process with me and opened my mind up to my past. A lot of memories I forgot, and some I pushed aside on purpose. I appreciate your help and you shining a light on even the darkest times. I truly was reminded to never forget my past…no matter how ugly it was.

Thank you to my team members who I've had in the last 10 years: Keith, Athena, Audrey, Mary Lou, Mary, Mark, Carrie, Bob, Allen, Herb, and Brad. You all play such a valuable role in helping me achieve my very best. I humbly know that I did this on my own, but it was me running with your suggestions that gave me my success. Thank you so much. I will continue to use your advice and suggestions for myself and the people I work with.

Thank you, Mom. You supported me so much with my struggles and never left my side. After Dad died, you and I became a team together. We both were trying to figure life out. You as a widow and me as a young adult in this wild world. You, at times, needed to step away to protect yourself, and I understand that. I'm so glad that when you left, we had no secrets or resentments towards each other. I truly felt at peace when you died, and I am so happy that you are back with Dad now. Thanks for always being my biggest fan. I miss you.

Meg, my wonderful wife, you have been an amazing wall to lean against. You have been a great partner through life and helping set up my private practice, Rebos, and my day to day life. Thanks for always talking me through everything and telling me what I need to hear. You truly fill in where I am weak. I couldn't imagine having someone more supportive than you in my life. I honestly and humbly know that I wouldn't have half as much as I do now. I love you, and you are my best friend.

Finally, thank you, my brother Odie. You pulled me from a hell hole you didn't even understand how dark it really was. I had honestly given up on life, and the world was going to do whatever it wanted with me. For whatever reason, your words in that car still ring very clear, and I use them as a guide for the decisions I make for my future each day. Thanks, big brother. I deeply appreciate and love you.

Table of Contents

Foreword

The field for the treatment of substance use disorders is in a serious crisis...a crisis that has reached critical mass. In addition to clinical rigidity and other practices that create poor patient care, we are also seeing an unprecedented level of unethical practices involving patient brokering and other outrageous behavior like purchasing insurance for patients needing treatment and then paying them to enter treatment.

The current state of affairs is unacceptable. Something has to change. If we don't address these issues, and address them with the sense of urgency they deserve, then we are at risk of losing public confidence in treatment.

There are some treatment programs and members of the treatment community that are doing something about the mess that has been created. Ross is one of those individuals.

Maximum Strength reflects his outrage at the current state of affairs. You will sense his anger and frustration in the pages that follow. But he also goes far beyond just criticizing the field. He offers us, and most importantly, the person who is suffering from chronic relapse, guidelines for a solution. The solution he offers is rooted in his personal experience in recovery.

Emotional sobriety has recently taken its rightful place in recovery. In fact, you will not be able to enjoy full recovery without it. I've defined emotional sobriety as the state of mind that is achieved when the best of you is in charge of and speaks for the rest of you. Ross recognizes the importance of both physical sobriety and emotional sobriety and has laid out a way of approaching recovery that will help you put the best of you in charge of your life.

Recovery did not come easy for Ross. He relapsed many times before being able to lay a foundation for his long-term recovery. But in that process, he learned many valuable lessons—lessons that he shares with us in practical, down to earth advice. One of the many that stands out is, "Stop trying to find yourself and start creating yourself." I couldn't have said it better myself.

Allen Berger, Ph.D.

Clinical Director of the Institute for Optimal Recovery and Emotional Sobriety

Hazelden Author of *12 Stupid Things that Mess Up Recovery, 12 Smart Things to do When the Booze and Drugs are Gone, 12 Hidden Rewards of Making Amends,* and *12 More Stupid Things that Mess Up Recovery.*

Introduction

I am not a doctor. Not only am I not a doctor, but I don't want to be a doctor. I'm not a part of the vastly growing rehabilitation system either...nor do I want to be!

And my number one reason for not wanting any of that? It's become nothing but big business and politics.

Here's what I am.

I am a guy that chronically relapsed for decades, spending seven-figure sums of money on drugs and alcohol—and when no one could help me, I started helping myself. After all, the answers are out there, but there are so many myths and misunderstandings in the failing world of rehab that most people are set up to fail from the start. This more than hurts me; it downright angers and disturbs me.

Does it sound like I'm yelling at times?

Well, maybe I am. If you have seen what I have seen, you would know what I mean, and you'd understand why I'm not quiet about this. I'm doing my best to edit my obscenities to a minimum, but if you are looking for some cute book with clever ways to "overcome," this isn't it. The life of an addict is one of extremes. It's a life of abusing, stealing, and hurting people. And that's just what they do to their friends and family. From there it gets worse.

You should be reading this book for two reasons:

1. You have tried on your own and through others to go straight. You have tried and failed. Sure, maybe you go

clean for a while, but it just doesn't stick for whatever reason. You're stuck. You're in trouble, or you're about to be in serious trouble. You have cheated death. Some, if not all, of your friends and family have started giving up on you, and you keep finding a new rock bottom.

2. You have a friend or family member that fits the above description, and you're ready to try something different, something better, something that is maximum strength and not some bureaucracy more worried about their bottom line. You truly want to help them, and you don't know how—but you are teachable enough to try something different, because the person you love is different. And because they're worth it.

Addiction is ugly—and I've been there

The week before my last stay at rehab, I went to jail for defrauding a casino.

I remember not being able to drink water because I was all cuffed up: my head down to my waist, going through my ankles to my wrists, were all in chains. So alone, pissed, shackled, and thirsty, I began to think that I was, in fact, insane. After all, the cops would not even unlock me from the chains even though I was locked inside the holding cell. This confirmed my thought. I was insane.

I had been sleeping on my couch with my shields down when the inevitable happened…I was arrested. In my warped perception, it wasn't so bad because I wasn't getting arrested at my drug dealer's house. That was a huge concern of mine, to get arrested at my dealer's house. See…insane.

I remember putting tinfoil on my windows. I turned my peephole inside out. If the paratroopers were coming to get me, I wanted to see them first.

2

I had been awake for thirteen days straight (my no-sleep record, actually). I was sure the paratroopers were coming though my window followed by a SEAL team. Every government and military agency was waiting to take me down for the crimes I committed against myself. This delusional thinking and paranoid manifestation was not only a result of my prolonged drug use but also a good indication that I was not in my right mind. Anyone that has over indulged in mind-altering substances may be able to relate to this thought: "They are coming to get me." Who they are, where they come from, what they are looking for, and how they found me are always unanswered questions.

To this day, I don't know who they are, but I believed—I *knew*, just like I know I have ten fingers and ten toes—that they were indeed out there looking for me, and that they were coming to get me to take me to where they came from. Wherever that is, I again have no idea.

Of course, this time 'they' did come for me, and then I was shackled and behind bars.

It's not easy, but it is possible

Believe me when I tell you that I understand what you may be going though. I'm not one of these guys that doesn't understand what the hell you are going though. That is the whole point of all of this: my work as an addiction counselor and advocate, this book, any talk I give. I've lived and experienced a true hell of my own creation, and I did not die. I found a way to change, transform my life, and come out on the other side.

It might not be easy, but it sure is possible. Seriously, if I can do it, anyone can. No question.

Almost every time I went to treatment, it was because I wanted to. I would literally drive there myself, pay for it myself, the whole bit. But wanting to change and actually making changes are two very different things. Saying, "I want to lose 20 pounds" is just worthless mouth movement without actual action. Going to the gym and eating right day in and day out is a different story. *Doing the work* - that's the only way to achieve the goal.

Nothing changed until I shut up and just did the work, day in and day out. I still do the work day in and day out. Don't lie to yourself. There is no other way. All those other times, it was as if I was sitting in a corner telling myself I was going to lose 20 pounds, and never getting up off my ass.

I ended up going to eight different inpatient treatment programs before sobriety stuck for me. A lot of that had to do with what I was bringing (or not bringing) to the table, but much of it also came from the failures of the treatment industry.

The treatment industry, as it exists today, fails 95% of the people who come through it. That is not a good track record.

In all my time doing inpatient and outpatient programs, I saw what worked—and what didn't work. And I'm not talking from a theoretical perspective; I'm talking from a lived perspective. I saw what worked and what didn't work *for me*, a hardcore addict. I saw what worked and what didn't work for other addicts like me, other addicts like you, or addicts like the person you love who's fighting addiction.

I'm writing this book to help make sure you don't have to bounce back and forth between treatment and relapse for years like I did—or worse, end up as just another overdose-death statistic. There are a lot of problems in the treatment industry, but addiction recovery *can work*. It can work for you. And I'm going to help show you how.

This book is about addiction recovery—and so much more

Before we really jump in, let's clear something up: addiction recovery is about way more than just addiction.

4

Yes, everything in this book is here to help you or your loved one stop drinking, doing drugs, gambling, or whatever your addiction is. But all of these skills and practices really boil down to how to live a successful life. Even if you're reading this book because someone you love is fighting addiction, there's a lot here that you can apply too. And when you do, you're going to find your life soaring to new heights. If you've ever struggled to lose weight, get your finances under control, or create better relationships with your family—everything in here can help you make that happen.

Even though the road might be rocky at times, I'm going to let you in on a little secret—it can be fun too. Creating an awesome life is, in fact, a whole lot of fun.

So, buckle up, strap in, and get ready for the best adventure you've ever had.

PART ONE

Extreme Recovery

Chapter One
The #1 Reason Why
You Can't Currently Recover

The first time I went to an addiction treatment center, I was a strung-out mess. I walk in the door, and I'm suddenly in this huge place with a gajillion people hustling around. I go up to the intake desk, desperate for someone to see me, help me, get me out of this hell…and then I get a bunch of paperwork, a stack of books, and a room.

I'm being shuffled around, just another patient in a sea of patients. And with the industry's 95% failure rate, let's be honest, I'm just another patient in a sea of patients who no one really expects to succeed. Sure, they're hoping I get this monkey off my back, and they want to help me do that, but truth be told they're statistically 95% sure I won't. And it shows in the standard treatment.

I didn't really have someone assigned to me in a particular one-on-one way, no specialist dedicated to checking in on me and supporting me in the treatment program. I *technically* had someone assigned to me, but in the 30 days that I was there, I met with them for a total of 42 minutes.

Forty-two minutes in 30 days. Do the math, and that breaks down to 84 seconds per day. Eighty-four seconds per day of one-on-one check-ins with the person "assigned" to me. I'm putting some really big quotes around "assigned" there, because you and I both know that 84 seconds per day means exactly jack shit.

And they wonder why the failure rate is 95%?

The final time that I went into treatment, I had four or five specialists working with me throughout my time there, addressing the four or five parts of me that needed to be realigned and recalibrated. There was actually an intentional awareness of what exactly was going on with me and what needed fixing. It started to seem like this guy named Ross was in treatment, not just Patient #37629.

And I actually made it work.

If you're not receiving customized care, you're setting yourself up to fail

Now, before you freak out, 'customized care' doesn't have to mean tens of thousands of dollars every month. Bear with me here, and you'll find that whatever your means, 'custom care' is well within your reach, right now.

'Custom care' really means that someone has identified what exactly is out of alignment with you and is implementing solutions that fit the problems. Simple as that.

And it makes sense, doesn't it?

If your car was out of whack, you wouldn't want to just park it in a mechanic's shop and hope the problem fixed itself. You wouldn't want to give it to a mechanic who didn't even look at it but said, "I'll give it an oil change, fresh coat of paint, and rotate the tires. It's what I do for everyone, and it fails 95% of the time, but it's the best I can do."

No. That mechanic is crap. You would want to take it to a mechanic who would put your car through some serious diagnostic check-ups, figure out what's going on with it, and fix the actual problems your car has. Obviously.

But apparently, it's not so obvious in the treatment industry. So, what do you do?

If you want a solution that works, you have to find one that fits the problem.

Customized care can mean different things in different cases

The first possibility is, of course, to find a treatment center that is centered on this philosophy. When I do treatment, this is exactly what we do; we work with the patients to figure out what issues they're dealing with—physiologically, mentally, and emotionally—and we get specialists on their team to help them.

But what do you do if you can't afford a world-class treatment center? Or if you're dealing with an addiction that doesn't really fit that sort of treatment, like an addiction to gambling or porn?

Again, it's all about creating customized care. Identify the specific issues at play, and execute a plan to fix them.

Identifying those issues could mean working with trained professionals, but it could also mean you working with books like this to self-identifying what's going on (and what's going wrong). When it comes to doing the actual work, that can entail a whole variety of action steps. If you identify personal accountability as a vital gap for you, it could mean finding an accountability program or partner that suits the addiction you're fighting with. If you realize that your addiction is thriving in your self-imposed isolation, it could mean you regularly attending AA or other relevant meetings to get yourself working in a community. Custom-care work can also mean working through home-study courses that are specifically geared towards the addictions and issues you're struggling with.

Whatever your monetary means, and whatever your addiction, customized care is the make-or-break point when it comes to getting that monkey off your back.

Imagine the standard treatment philosophy as a gym. People come with different goals and needs—lose 20 pounds, work on my heart health, look ripped on the beach, whatever—but everyone just gets thrown into a huge gym to figure it out. These people don't know how to work the machines, don't know a dumbbell from a barbell, don't know the difference between sets and repetitions, and are just expected to make it work.

If you want to lose 20 pounds, you need to know how to actually do that. What exercises to do, what machines to use, how to do all of that safely and effectively, how to incorporate nutrition into your program, and so on. And all of that's going to be different for someone who joins a gym with the goal of increasing their heart health. Different needs, different action steps.

Now, one great option is to hire a personal trainer who is educated in understanding what will best accomplish your goals, a nutritionist to develop a diet suited to your needs and your body type, a personal chef to prepare those meals, and a massage therapist to work on your body in between workouts, et cetera et cetera. If that's all within your means, fantastic. If you put the work in, you're going to see some amazing results.

But you don't need all of that to succeed in your goals at the gym. You can do much of the work yourself by finding reputable books that teach you how to do exercises safely, a workout program specifically geared towards your goals with a track record of success, and information about healthy nutrition. Even with this self-directed custom care, if you put the work in, you're going to see results.

Same with addiction.

Throughout this book, I'm going to present you with tons of opportunities to start developing your customized care. We're going to break down what addiction is, what sobriety is, common failure points, strategies for relapse prevention—the whole nine yards. As you read, actively be on the lookout for where your personal gaps are, where you need to focus energy and attention, and what strategies will address those precise issues. Whether you then take this empowered knowledge into a treatment center or into self-directed care, it's going to exponentially increase your recovery potential.

Customize your care, do the work, see results. Simple as that.

Chapter Two
For Friends & Family Only

Before we get any further into this book, I want to take a chapter to speak directly to the friends and families of addicts.

A lot of you reading this book have picked it up because you yourselves are struggling with addiction. If that's you, skip this chapter and move right on to Chapter Three—I'll see you there.

The rest of you have picked this book up because someone else in your life is struggling with addiction—which means, in your own way, you're struggling with addiction too. Maybe it's your son or daughter who's slid from high school parties into prescription pill abuse; maybe your husband or wife is drinking a full six-pack or bottle of wine every night; maybe one of your dear friends is pouring their money and life into slot machines, cocaine, sex and prostitutes, or any of the thousand other things that addiction can latch onto.

This chapter is for you.

You're in the fight against addiction too

Firstly, I want to acknowledge you for seeking out this book—for looking for resources that could help this person struggling in your life. It shows character, compassion, grit, and commitment. Whoever the addict is in your life, she or he is lucky to have you—whether or not they realize it.

Which brings me to the next point. Speaking from experience, let me say it loud and clear—addicts can be real assholes.

When addiction has its grip on us, good people can turn to lies, theft, avoidance, you name it. You've likely found it tough to confront your loved one about their addiction, getting only defensiveness and resistance in return. If your loved one is deep in the shit, it might seem like you hardly recognize them anymore.

It's ok for you to feel frustrated, angry, even hopeless at times. In fact, it's not just ok; it's a perfectly human response. Oftentimes, the family and friends struggle with ambivalence when it comes to the addict in their lives. Ambivalence means you're pulled in two directions—on the one hand you desperately want to help, and on the other hand part of you just wants to avoid the issue and push the person away. That's natural.

Truth is, when someone is fighting addiction, they're not the only ones in the fight. They take their friends and family with them. Addiction has thrown your life into turmoil too. Odds are, it sometimes keeps you up at night. You might not have the junk in your system, but you're right there in the trenches with the addict you love.

Addiction is a disease that affects everyone around the addict.

You make a difference

The upside to that is that when you're in the trenches, you've got an arsenal at your command too.

15

Even if you sometimes feel hopeless, it's vital that you realize you *do* make a difference. When you fight addiction—which is different than fighting the addict—you're pulling your loved one out of the muck and mire.

Research consistently shows that friends and family are often a huge factor both in getting addicts into treatment and making recovery work. In my own case, the last time I went to a rehab treatment center, my brother literally dragged my ass there. If it weren't for my family's commitment to my recovery, I would not be here. I'd be six feet under, good for nothing but worm food. My family and friends got me here. You can get your loved one onto a better path too.

You've also got to keep in mind that when you help yourself, you're helping the addict you love too. My council for anyone working with a suffering addict is to first and foremost take care of yourself. When you feel like you're always running on an empty tank, or you're just overwhelmed by the negative impact addiction is having on *your* life, it only makes it harder for you to play a positive role in the life of the addict you love.

Also, remember that you can lead a horse to water, but you can't make them drink. You can't singlehandedly cure addiction in someone else. They have to be open to a new way of living, and the treatment they receive is responsible for leading them down that path. It's up to you to play a supportive role, to be understanding or give some tough-love as needed, but it doesn't serve anyone for you to think that the entire burden is on your shoulders. No one needs you to be a martyr to addiction.

The best thing I ever learned as a counselor is to make sure that the first thing I say to a new client walking in is, "How can I help you?" The philosophy that I've found most critical to working with addicts is to meet them where they're at. Addicts come in as emotional and physical wrecks, and it's our job to help them. Not toss them under a pile of books, not feed them into a generic one-size-fits-all routine—meet them where they're at, and help them choose the next step of recovery each and every day.

This can be tough when the addict is someone you love. Sometimes you'll just want to shake—or smack—some sense into your friend. If only it worked that way. Personal connection, compassion, and commitment are your greatest weapons against addiction. There is no one-size-fits-all solution, no magic pill to shove down an addict's throat to make it all better. But when you're in the fight with them, the addict you love has way better odds of success.

How to use this book

Throughout much of this book, I'll sometimes be writing directly to an addict reader and other times addressing the friends and family in their life. But even when I'm 'talking to' an addict, I'm talking to you too.

As you read this book, you're going to gain massive insights into what the hell is going on with your loved one—the areas where they're likely misaligned, and strategies for them to recalibrate and live a lifelong recovery.

This understanding will empower you to more effectively take a stand for the addict in your life. You'll want to keep an ear out for what rings true in your particular case. Is your addict partner lacking accountability, or struggling with emotional sobriety, or continually relapsing in the "honeymoon" stage of recovery? All of that is vital knowledge to help them break through. When I talk about strategies for recovery, I'm also talking about ways that you can support addicts in recovering.

Remember, you make a difference. And with what I'm going to share with you in this book, you can make an exponentially greater difference. You're on Team Sobriety, and I'm right there with you. Let's do this.

Chapter Three
Building Your Dream Team

Let me take you back to May of 2007.

I'd just gotten out of jail (it's funny how many addict stories start like that, isn't it?). As soon as I was out, my autopilot kicked on, and that sucker had one mission: get drugs, get high. Find some drugs and some fellow druggies to keep me company. Go wild with it until I was passed out or dead.

When the knock at the door came, I naturally thought it was the guy bringing the drugs. Nope—I looked through the peephole and saw my brother standing there.

Now, my brother is a guy who has never taken a drug or drink in his entire life. And here I am with two girls and two guys in my house, all on the same get-drugs-get-high mission, none of whose last names I knew…clearly some quality friends of mine.

I opened the door and my brother said, "I heard you need some help."

I broke down and started bawling.

We got in his car, and I immediately started ranting about how I was really going to handle it this time. I figured he was going to throw me out the window and just kick the ever-loving tar out of me, but I couldn't help it. Addicts are like that, primo bullshit artists who just can't help themselves.

He looked at me and said, "I'm in a great marriage with a loving wife. I have four awesome kids who don't get into trouble. I don't drink, don't do drugs, and my dog comes when I call him.

I think I know a little bit more about life than you do right now, and I think that at the moment you're the last person to be questioning anything that comes out of my mouth."

He was right. We drove to a treatment center, and I checked in.

Happy ending? Not really. Three weeks later, I bailed from that rehab clinic. No notice, just straight AWOL.

Fast forward a few days, and I'm holed up again, cooking $3,000 worth of coke.

That sort of rehab-relapse bouncing back and forth probably sounds familiar to a lot of you reading this. Either you've been bouncing back and forth or an addict you know has been.

So, what would finally make the difference?

Building my sobriety team.

If you want to make it work, don't try to do it alone.

Sobriety is not a single-player game

The last time I went to treatment, I saw the power of a well-targeted sobriety team. I had four or five specialists working with me at any given time, each specifically trained to deal with a particular issue I was facing.

Whether or not you go to an inpatient treatment center, you've got to create your own sobriety team.

Imagine yourself as the president of a business—let's call it Your Great Sober Life, Inc. When you're an addict, the business of your life is spiritually bankrupt. Our job is to make you spiritually profitable on a daily basis.

In a thriving business, is the president the go-to person for every little thing? Of course not. They have a CEO, COO, and CFO; marketing directors and personnel directors; consultants and technicians, and a board of directors that oversees decision-making. The president is the head honcho, but a successful company president brings on experts, takes in their input and feedback, and acts accordingly.

You've got to follow that model in building the business of your life.

In my case, I've got a spiritual coach and a business coach. My wife is the expert I go to for anything in my personal life. My extended family are like outside consultants whose expertise and knowledge I draw on in specific scenarios.

I live my life in consultation. I'm humble enough to recognize that I'm not an expert in everything—far from it. So, I get input from my team, and I listen to it.

Finding and building your team

In your life of recovery, you need to have a team like this.

It's going to look different in every case, depending on the circumstances. My team started with a crew of specialists in a rehab center. It might be similar for you. But if that doesn't fit your situation, or is outside of your means, you get to build a different sort of team.

The core idea here is to find people and resources that are strong in areas that you're weak. Then listen to their input, and apply it.

First, you'll want to create a list of areas that you're not performing at 100%. Finances? Family relationships? Career?

Romantic relationships? What specific addiction problems are you having? Gambling? Opiates? Booze? As you go through this book, also identify where else you're having breakdowns. Emotional sobriety? Accountability?

With a list like this, the next step is to find team members you can bring on who are experts in the field. Some of these may already be people in your life, like how my wife is my go-to expert in my personal life. Some of these might mean bringing in new people like a therapist, AA sponsor, or life coach. Some of these might be other resources specifically geared toward areas of your life—like a financial management program or an addiction home-study course.

This is one of those areas of addiction recovery that mirrors the rest of life. No matter what your goals are in life, if you surround yourself with a top-notch support team, your odds of success skyrocket. If you want to lose weight and get in shape, sure, you could just go to a gym and wing it. Or you could hire a personal trainer, a nutritionist, and an accountability coach. You could go to the gym alone every time, or you could find yourself a gym buddy to make workouts more fun (and make it that much harder for you to bail on them). Which choices do you think will set you up for success?

We're stronger together, and collaboration creates success. It's no different with the journey of sobriety.

Remember, the goal is to make the business of your life spiritually profitable every day. A thriving business means a well-tuned team of experts. Your ticket to lifelong sobriety is the team that you build around you.

Humans are deeply social creatures, and we fly or die based on the people we surround ourselves with. So, let's build you a team that works for you.

Chapter Four
Quit the Lies First

Before we can start getting the real work done, there's something you and I need to get out in the open, dear reader.

Addicts are, through and through, bullshit artists.

Addicted brains lie. They love to lie. Addicts lie to themselves and lie to pretty much everyone else too. They lie about being in control, lie about how it's not a problem and "I can manage it, really!" Sometimes addicted brains lie for no real reason at all. Habits are like that.

If you're reading this as a friend or family member of an addict, odds are you know exactly what I mean. You're probably sick and tired of your loved one lying to you.

If you're reading this while stuck in addiction yourself, there's a good chance you're grimacing and nodding along with me. If you disagree, odds are you're lying to yourself right now.

And before you can quit your drug of choice for good, first you've got to quit the bullshit.

No, really, I'm a bullfighter

Trust me, I was no exception to this rule.

When I was wrapped up in addiction, everything out of my mouth—every sentence, thought, and word that I uttered to people—was an outright, 100% lie.

If you lived in a three-bedroom house, I would tell you I lived in a four-bedroom house. Just because. If you had an eight-passenger plane, I would tell you that I had a nine-and-a-half passenger plane. If you smoked three 8-balls a day, I smoked six. I used to tell people that I owned a nightclub in Chicago.

Just to set the record straight, I would like to officially state that I do not own a plane, nor have I ever owned a plane in the past. If I ever offered to fly you somewhere in said plane, let me again state that such plane never, in fact, existed. I also definitely did not own a nightclub in Chicago. Let the record show that I was, in fact, completely full of shit.

I think back to the girls I would meet before Meg entered my life. My big hangout was the Hyatt Casino at Incline Village in Lake Tahoe. I was there all the time. The bartender used to say, "Ross, I can't wait until some woman sits next to you so I can hear what comes out of your mouth today, because it's always a riot."

Sometimes I'd tell people I was an amateur bullfighter in Reno. Seriously. The bartender knew I was completely full of it, 100% of the time, but at least I put on a good show.

But really, that was how I was living my life. Full of crap, spouting lies and outright fantasy, trying to put on a good show for whoever was in front of me.

And it wasn't just for strangers either. I created different Rosses, different fantasy versions of myself to suit each need. I was one Ross with my mother and a different Ross with my brother. I was different versions of myself with each of my sisters, my Lake Tahoe friends, my Chicago friends, my Wisconsin friends. Hell, I even had a 'rehab Ross' ready to go for when I went to treatment.

There were dozens of versions of myself, each distinct and separate versions of "me." Looking back, it's not surprising I started using. It was exhausting keeping all those different versions of myself straight in my head. And I never even got a single Oscar nomination.

I lied for a living. I did it well, because that's what we do. Addicts lie. We just do. We lie because we are scared that you'll see who we really are and not like us. The lie is the mask that we wear. The "real" person inside is numbed out with our drug of choice, hiding out of sight, and slowly dying.

When you let yourself tell lies, you lose your integrity. When you lose your integrity, you lose yourself.

Recovery means getting real

Again, let's not mince words. If you want to beat your addiction, you've got to quit the bullshit.

It's pretty common for anyone to play slightly different versions of themselves in different situations, but addicts go way overboard. Way, way overboard.

If you want to fix any problem, you've got to first see and understand the problem clearly. If you're still swimming in a swamp of lies, you're not going to see anything clearly, and you're not going to get anywhere.

Again, I wasn't any exception here. A few weeks into my final inpatient treatment program, I found myself sitting around a table with other clients, all of us smoking cigarettes and talking. And just like in the outside world, pretty much everything that came out of my mouth was a lie. Back at my room, I had this epiphany about how addicted I was to lying and bullshitting. So, at that moment, I decided to just shut up. I would still talk with counselors and therapists and staff, but I completely stopped talking to other clients—for weeks. I would eat by myself, sit by myself. I stopped hanging out at the smokers' table. I needed that silence to start to break my dependence on lies.

If you're still wrapped up in your addiction, it might seem daunting to actually start telling the truth—even (or maybe especially) to yourself. Maybe you've been living in Fantasy Valley so long that you don't even know who your 'true self' is anymore. Sometimes addicts just get lost in the lies, and it's hard to see the way out.

I'm going to walk you through the process in this book, but I can't do the work for you. If you're committed to the lies and masks and self-deception and the pretending-it's-not-a-big-deal, then you might as well put this book down now. Give it to someone who's willing to get real, get honest, and do the work.

But, if *you're* the one who's willing to get real, get honest, and do the work, then buckle up, buddy. I've been where you are now, and I know how awful it can feel at first to start taking all those masks off and to start getting honest with yourself. But let me tell you that it is worth it. Having a life that you can truly be happy with is worth it. Having genuine, honest relationships with the people you love is worth it. Sobriety is worth it.

Chapter Five

Think Like a Business: Take it Quarterly

When you're in the business of building a sober life, it pays to think about things just like that—a business.

A business is designed to create something valuable, whether a product or service, and profit financially. In your own thinking, you're working towards creating a valuable life—a life that you can look back on and be proud of, a life that brings you joy and fulfillment through all its ups and downs.

Just like a business, you want to be profitable. But whereas a normal business aims to be financially profitable, you'll want to aim for what I call being *spiritually profitable*.

Being spiritually profitable is about creating forward progress on a life that works. It's about learning to love yourself. It's about getting in sync with life—having a career that fulfills you, relationships where you can be your honest self. It's about having fun, being able to laugh, being able to cry when things get tough or sad. It's about living life, genuinely.

That's a big part of what this whole sobriety journey is about. When you're stuck in addiction, you're not spiritually profitable. You're probably falling deeper and deeper into spiritual debt—relationships falling apart, hating yourself, all that great stuff. I've been there, and I know how it sucks. I'm here to help you shift out of that.

Think about time like a business does

One of the most productive ways to apply this analogy of thinking of your life like a business is when it comes to thinking about time. When it comes to time and sobriety, there are a few big pitfalls. One, which we'll get into more detail with later in this book, is the tendency for addicts to count *down*. As in, counting down the days until a 28-day rehab treatment is done, or counting down the days until they drag themselves past the one-year mark, and so on. We'll dig into this in more detail later, but suffice it so say, this doesn't work.

Another pitfall, which we discussed in the last chapter, is the pressure to feel like when you first approach sobriety, you need to be committed to being sober for the rest of your life. Do you think most businesses start this way? Do you think the average small-business owner first opened shop thinking, "I'm going to be doing this for the next 60 years, then my children and grandchildren will take over after me"?

Probably not. That would be sort of crazy thinking for someone first attempting a new business venture. Sure, you might well *hope* that this new business launches into a huge multinational business that runs through the next century, but that's not where you're really going to focus your attention and thinking.

Most businesses start out with someone saying, "Hey, I think this is a great idea for a business. I think I'd enjoy the work, I think it'd create a valuable product, and I think it would be profitable. Let's give it a try and see what happens."

Despite what most people think, that's the sort of thinking that gets a whole lot of people on the road to lifelong sobriety. I know that was true for me.

There's another pitfall that complements the "for the rest of your life and forever" danger. This one is the idea that you should just "take things one day at a time."

Here's the problem with taking it "one day at a time." At some point, you're going to have a really crappy day. A day where sobriety seems stupid, all the work you've put in feels pointless, and you just want to dive back into a mountain of cocaine (or whatever your addiction is).

If you're really taking it just "one day at a time," what's going to stop you from deciding, "Well, today has been crap, and I don't want to do this sobriety thing anymore,"?

I've seen way too many people throw away 50, 60, 70 days sober, just because they had one bad hour. One bad interaction. One morning fight with their spouse, and all that sobriety work gets flushed down the toilet. This "one day at a time" thinking makes this sort of breakdown all the more risky.

And I'll be honest with you here—this is something I've fallen victim to myself. Remember, I went into eight different treatment centers, so I've dealt with more than my share of relapses. So often, it would be just one bad decision after one bad day that would toss me right back into the trenches of addiction. It was only when I learned to start thinking bigger—and more stable—than just "one day at a time" that I was able to continue living relapse-free.

> # Your goal is to become spiritually profitable. Learn from how businesses become financially profitable.

Taking it quarterly

So, that all doesn't work. But what does work?

Well, what do successful businesses do?

They take things quarterly—in quarter-year chunks, three months at a time.

This is the strategy that works best to create successful, financially profitable businesses, and it's also the best strategy for you to create a spiritually profitable life.

Take your sobriety in 90-day chunks. If you're currently in the midst of your addiction and are considering first starting treatment and trying on the sober life, great. Commit to 90 days. No matter what happens, you're in-it-to-win-it for the next 90 days.

At the end of that 90-day period, do exactly what a successful business does. Sit down and evaluate the last quarter. A business will ask, "Have we been financially profitable?" You're going to ask, "Have I been spiritually profitable in the last 90 days? Do I feel like my life is on a better track now than it was 90 days ago? Have I grown personally in the last 90 days? Have my relationships been improving over the last 90 days?"

If you're answering yes to any of these questions, great! You've made a spiritual profit.

Now ask yourself this: if a business has their quarterly evaluation and discovers they made $100,000 last month, do you think they'll then decide to close up shop? They made some good money, so are they going to be satisfied with that and throw in the towel?

No. Of course not.

When a business is profitable, it keeps on moving forward, figuring out how to continue being profitable. Maybe even how to create *more* profit next quarter than was made the last quarter, right?

Take your life like this too.

Have you been spiritually profitable in the last 90 days of sobriety? Great! Commit to another 90 days—another 90 days of all-in sobriety, even if some days, or even some weeks, are really crappy. You're committed to another 90 days, no matter what.

Now let's take it further.

Sometimes, businesses aren't profitable. They lose money, they don't have reasonable plans to start turning a profit. So, what do they do? They close down.

If you ever reach a point where you think, "You know what? My life was way better when I was a raging crackhead. My relationships were better, I felt better about myself, I was more in sync with the world. Sobriety has not been spiritually profitable for me," then by all means, close shop on sobriety.

I'll be honest though, I don't really think you're ever going to do a quarterly evaluation and decide that the last 90 days of sobriety *wasn't* worth it. Because sobriety just has a tendency to create a more spiritually profitable life than addiction does. But hey, don't take my word for it. Commit to your first 90 days, and see for yourself.

Chapter Six
The Do's and Don'ts
Before Treatment

The 'common sense' around addiction and addiction treatment can be a double-edged sword. There are a lot of ideas that have been floating around our cultural consciousness for the last 50 or so years that just don't hold up to empirical evidence or scientific scrutiny. But like so much of the treatment industry today, these ideas just go unquestioned, despite the half-century of addiction research.

When you're considering heading into treatment, there are some common-knowledge ideas that can really mess things up. And there's one vital necessity that you have to be on-board with, or else you might as well not go.

There is no rock bottom

One of the most common ideas about addiction treatment is that before an addict can really start turning their life around, they have to hit 'rock bottom.'

Now let's take this idea apart a little bit.

The idea of 'rock bottom' suggests that there's some lowest of the lows that you can hit in life. That at some point, addiction will have screwed up your life so damn much, that there's no further down it could take you. You're at the absolute bottom, and *then* (and only then) you can start to turn your life around.

Now really, does that make any sense at all?

Is it true *anywhere* in life that at some point things just couldn't possibly get worse?

Of course not.

Take your relationships. What does 'worst case scenario' sound like? Maybe your spouse leaving you and your family telling you you're just a complete failure in life. That sounds pretty wretched. But could it get worse? What if you had kids with your spouse and the courts decided that you weren't allowed to see them? What if your family told you they didn't want you coming around anymore?

Could it get any worse than that?

What if, before they left, your kids told you that they were relieved that they'd never have to see you again? What if your parents got a literal restraining order against you?

It might seem like a grim sort of mind-game, but the reality is that things can always be worse. And if you let it, addiction will take you into depths of 'worse and worse' that you never could have imagined possible.

When I was first getting into partying, drugs, and alcohol, I would never have imagined the awful depths that addiction would take my life to. If you had asked me when I was 20 years old whether being a full-fledged, spoon-cooking crackhead would be my 'rock bottom,' my eyes would have bugged out of my head. "Rock bottom?!" I would have said, "I think my 'rock bottom' would be way before that. No way would it get to that level."

Well guess what: it got even worse for me.

When I was in my mid-20's, if you had asked me if getting arrested multiple times in a single week would have been my 'rock bottom,' I would have had the same reaction. But again—addiction took me that low, and even further down.

When I talk with clients and their families, I describe addiction as a hole that you're in. You've got a really strong and sharp shovel with you in that hole. The deeper you dig yourself, the sharper that shovel gets. So, no matter how deep of a hole you dig yourself in, you'll always be able to dig yourself even farther down.

You know what 'rock bottom' *really* is?

Death.

Dying from overdose, or freezing to death, homeless in the streets. That's rock bottom. When addiction literally kills you—like it kills hundreds of people in this country every day.

But guess what?

There aren't a lot of treatment options once you're dead.

I cringe when I hear friends or family of addicts—or addicts themselves—talking about how they just need to let someone hit rock bottom before they try to get them the help they need. This is insane.

If you're waiting for someone to dig themselves down to 'rock bottom,' you're literally just letting them dig their own grave.

You don't have to be committed to lifelong sobriety

There's a common notion that for treatment to work, for rehab to actually make any difference in an addict's life, the addict has to go in committed to giving up their drugs or booze for good. For life. After all, if they aren't committed to never touching the addiction again, then they're never going to be sober, right?

Wrong.

This one tends to get a more resistant reaction, even from some people in the treatment industry. But more than industry professionals, even suggesting this tends to send family and friends of addicts up the wall. These people see their loved one's life falling apart thanks to addiction. They want the addict to get clean, period. To get their life back together, to start actually living it.

When someone suggests that an addict should approach treatment with anything less than a commitment to lifelong sobriety, all that these friends and family members can hear is, "They're eventually going to fall right back into their old ways."

But addiction recovery isn't a light switch that just flips on and off. It's a dimmer switch.

I'll let you in on a little secret. When I went to a treatment center for the last time, I had no plans to stop doing cocaine for the rest of my life. That idea would have been incomprehensible to me. No freaking way.

But, I knew full well that my drug habits were wrecking my life. I saw my life in shambles. I knew that I was on the verge of losing any relationship with my family for good. I knew I wanted something to change.

So, I thought, "You know what? I'll give this a try. See what it's like to not do coke for a while, and try to get my head on straight."

Even after I was through my detox and getting into the real work of sobriety, I didn't think I'd be drug-free for the rest of my life.

Instead, I would take it piece by piece.

After a few months of sobriety, I looked back on my life and saw that things had gotten better. I was becoming spiritually profitable. So, hey, let's give it another three months, and see what that's like. Even at this point, thinking about a lifetime of sobriety sounded insane. I couldn't imagine saying "I'm never going to do coke again for the rest of my life" or "I'm never going to have another drink as long as I live." But as time went on, I could imagine more and more of a sober future.

For a long time, "lifelong sobriety" sounded insane to me. I was doing the work, creating huge progress within myself, all that good stuff, but I still could only think about sobriety as something I was doing for a finite period of time.

When I was one year sober, I went out to dinner with some friends. One of them asked me if I was going to go for another year sober. I said, "Yes. The last year was definitely worth it. It was hell at times, but it was worth it."

Another year later, I was asked the same question. At that point, I could imagine sobriety even further out, and said that I'd do two more years. When I got to two and a half years sober, I remember sitting one day and asking myself how far out I could really imagine being sober. I could picture myself being sober for five years at that point.

Just six months later, at three years into my sobriety, I was 32 years old. I realized, at that point, that it didn't scare me to say I'd be sober for another 10 years. Then I asked myself, "Does it scare me to think about being sober for the next 20 years?" I would be 52 at that point. It didn't scare me to think about being sober for the next 20 years, and 20 years pretty much felt like a lifetime. After all, do I really want to be a 52-year old dude who starts blowing cocaine again?

Maybe this *is* just going to be something I do for the rest of my life.

That was the first moment that I really felt like I could be in this for the rest of my life. The first time I could think about being sober for the rest of my life.

And remember, this was when I already had three solid years of sobriety under my belt.

If you're an addict, or you have an addict in your life, you've got to understand: considering lifelong sobriety while in the trenches of addiction is usually impossible.

Imagine your five favorite foods, five favorite activities, and five favorite people in your life. Now, imagine a doctor telling you that if you want to be healthy, you need to never eat any of those foods, do any of those activities, or see any of those people…for the rest of your life. That would sound inconceivable. No way.

That's what these substances or habits are like for hardcore addicts. They're what they wake up for, what they scrounge up money for, what they live for. Until they start replacing drugs or booze or whatever with real sources of joy and fulfillment, it's outrageous to imagine *never* doing them again. What would there be to live for?

So, whether you're an addict or there's an addict in your life: don't wait for them to decide they're ready for lifelong sobriety. It's a fool's errand. Get them in the game, and have them start *seeing* the benefits of sobriety. Then, piece by piece, they'll go forward with it. Another three months. Another six months. Another year, then five years, then ten.

Before you know it, sobriety sticks for good.

You've got to be in the game 100%. Anything less is just waiting to fail.

What you *do* need going in

Before going into treatment, you *don't* need to hit some hypothetical 'rock bottom,' and you *don't* need to be committed to a lifetime of sobriety.

But there is one vital key that you need to have going in. Without this, treatment just isn't going to work.

You need to be committed to being open to new ideas. You need to accept that other people might have better ideas about how to live life.

There are parts of treatment programs that you might really not like. Maybe for you it's looking at your own inner issues, beyond the chemical dependency. Maybe it's talking to an individual counselor or doing group work. Maybe it's work with people in your life, like making amends.

Well, here's the thing—you can't just pick and choose the parts of treatment programs you're comfortable doing and expect that to be good enough.

You can't be open to just half of treatment, and expect to end up sober. You can't even expect to end up half sober—you'll just wind up right back in the addiction. Even doing 90% won't cut it. It's an all-or-nothing game here, folks.

It's like cancer. Imagine you rid yourself of 99% of the cancer in your body. Ninety-nine percent is pretty good, right? Maybe 99% healthy sounds good enough to you.

But we all know what's going to happen. That 1% remaining will grow, spread, metastasize, and before you know it, your body is ridden with cancer again.

Addiction is the same way. You need to hit it from all angles to actually get a grip on it. You can't half-ass this.

Part of being completely open in treatment is not throwing anything away. Everything that comes at you while you're in treatment, take it in.

Some ideas or stories or encouragements might not seem earth-shattering to you at the moment you hear them. Some of them will fall flat on your ears. Some might sound weird, but however you feel about them in the moment, don't throw them away. Take them in, and store them away. You never know when something you heard in the third week of your treatment will make all the difference in staying sober for your third year.

This is true even if you're not yet thinking about being sober for the rest of your life. That's fine. But if you've committed to giving this sobriety thing a shot for the next 90 days, you need to be *all in* for these next 90 days.

If you're not doing that, you're just setting yourself up to fail. If you *do* commit to being open to new ideas and taking in everything that's offered to you, you have a chance to turn this ship around and create a life that you're proud of.

Chapter Seven
Your First Quarter:
90 Days Inpatient

Ok, so as we discussed in the Chapter Five, you're going to think about sobriety in terms of 90-day quarters.

Not surprisingly, the first 90 days is probably the most important. This is the time period that sets the standard for however long you're going to take this sober journey. A powerful, spiritually profitable first 90 days can set you up for lifelong sober success. On the flipside, a first 90 days of sub-par treatment will make it that much harder to keep the sobriety train rolling.

Unfortunately, these first 90 days are when the standard treatment industry seriously drops the ball.

The 90 days you should aim for

First, let's take a look at what this first 90 days of sobriety *should* look like. This is a realistic look at what you'd hope for.

To begin with, these first 90 days should be in an inpatient treatment center. Now, that's not the norm in the industry today, and we'll get into that more later in this chapter, but for now let's continue with what these 90 days of inpatient treatment *should* entail.

First, you're in detox.

Detox sucks. Your body is working the junk out of your system, and it is a wretched experience. We'll dive into this period more in the next chapter, but suffice it to say that detox and withdrawal are dire, sometimes life-threatening, crisis periods in addiction treatment.

You can expect detox to last the first few days to the first few weeks of these 90 days. During this time, you're in your own little wing of the treatment center. People are coming in to take your vitals and check on you pretty much constantly. The attention is intense, but it's pretty much all focused on physiologically treating your chemical dependency.

Let's say you move out of detox after about one week (the exact time will depend on your body and particular chemical dependency). Now you're moved into a new wing of the treatment center, which is basically an entirely new world. You're starting to meet with your counselor, you're starting to pick up the routine of this new branch of treatment, learning the schedule and how things work, and so on.

For these next few weeks, you're still incredibly raw from detox. You don't know anything about treatment at this point; you don't know your counselor from Adam—all you really know is that you blew *way* too much cocaine. These weeks are really a transition into the serious work of sobriety.

You're at the beginning here of some really intense, intimate relationships with your counselors. You may have already hired them, but you don't really know them yet—and you're about to start spilling your guts to them. You're going to be opening up to them about all the crazy, twisted shit that may be in your past. And that requires a level of trust that you have to build.

In this first month, you're building that trust. It's almost like a month of courting, building up this relationship with your counselors.

So now we've completed roughly the first month.

The second month is when you begin the real work of sobriety in earnest. You're now in sync with the program, starting to build community and camaraderie with the other addicts there. Your focus this month is to start digging into the underlying personal issues behind your addiction. This is done through a combination of group work and individual counseling.

In most treatment centers today, you'll encounter far too little individual counseling and far too much reliance on group work, just expecting addicts to read the literature, and figuring things out for themselves. But in an ideal first 90 days, you're spending this second month doing a lot of intensive work with your individual counselors.

This month is also when you start to really begin living without the emotional armor of your addiction. When you were an addict, you used your addiction to regulate your emotions. Feel bad? Get drunk. Want to feel happy? Do coke. Want to forget your problems? Shoot some smack.

Now you don't have those artificial regulators. In that first month, your body was in literal shock dealing with the absence of those chemicals. In this second month, you're starting to really deal with the emotional reality of not having those crutches. You'll probably physically and emotionally feel like one big exposed nerve—hyper-sensitive and raw to the touch. You're like a live wire, taking your first baby steps into learning how to live with your emotions organically.

In the third month of these 90 days, you're starting to really get some traction. You've been digging deep with your individual counselors, and you're starting to come to grips with the underlying issues you have going on. You're continuing to work on family stuff, relationship stuff, personal stuff. You're starting to figure out where you're going to live when you leave the inpatient center, making plans for the outside world. Wounds are starting to heal, amends are being made.

This is the month when you're preparing yourself for life after inpatient care. You're creating a stable foundation to continue the work outside of the treatment center's walls.

If you don't get the care you need, you won't have the success you deserve.

But the treatment industry today falls way short

There's probably no treatment center out there today that would deny that addicts should ideally spend their first 90 days of treatment in an inpatient center.

But, few addicts in treatment actually get those 90 days of inpatient care.

This is an example of how the standard treatment industry today is failing addicts. The trend over the last 50 years has been to offer less treatment, less one-on-one-work, and all of that in shorter lengths of time.

Even for centers that do treat addicts as inpatients for 90 days, what they do in those 90 days can be alarming. I know a lot of places where addicts would basically do everything either on their own or in group work. Places where you meet an individual counselor for at most once a week, for maybe 30 minutes each session. Here's the problem—everyone has issues and secrets and problems that just aren't going to come out in a shared circle of 15 strangers. Group work can be good for some things, but it cannot ever replace the value of individual, one-on-one counseling.

When I was a ski instructor, sometimes I would teach group lessons and other times I'd give one-on-one training. Whether I was working with an individual or a group, I'd be covering the same material, teaching the same techniques and skills. But I always found that what it would take me two whole days to teach a group of 10 people, would only take me half a day tops to teach a single student one-on-one.

Working one-on-one is just more effective. In a group, attention gets spread out, and you can only move as fast as the slowest person in the group.

On top of the problem of depersonalized care, most treatment centers these days aren't even keeping addicts as inpatients for anywhere close to 90 days.

Most addicts are leaving inpatient care after just 28 or 30 days—when all they've really addressed is chemical dependency. That is a recipe for failure, which is really no surprise, given the 95% failure rate in the industry today. Treatment centers these days are creating discharge plans for addicts who are still in detox. Insanity.

Unfortunately, things don't seem to be moving in a good direction. I've begun noticing an alarming trend lately. Insurance companies are starting to suggest that if someone is seeking treatment for the first time, maybe they should just *start* in an outpatient program. Then if that doesn't work, sure, we can put them into an inpatient program (for a few weeks, then the bill's on you, of course).

This is just heartless. Someone's dealing with a heroin addiction, so let's first try out the cheapest, most minimal level of treatment. And only if they fail with that and fuck things up again, will we give them real, inpatient care? This with something that kills hundreds of people every day. Honestly, it ends up cheaper for the insurance company if the addict just OD's and dies in this first 'trial period' of outpatient care.

Really makes you wonder where their priorities are.

It can sometimes feel like an uphill battle getting the inpatient care that you need, given the realities of the standard treatment industry. But knowing the roadmap going in will empower you to find the appropriate treatment programs that fit your needs. This knowledge will also help you supplement programs as needed—if you're not getting a lot of one-on-one counseling in your inpatient or outpatient program, then you know you need to bring on some additional counseling and therapy ASAP.

In the next chapters, we'll examine these first 90 days in more detail—including some huge relapse danger-zones that you need to be aware of.

Chapter Eight
Sobriety Starts at a Crisis Point

One of the biggest failures of the standard treatment industry is that they just don't meet addicts where they're at—and when treatment starts, addicts are at a major crisis point.

One of the pillars of the standard treatment industry is something called "The 12 Core Functions of a Substance Abuse Counselor[1]." These supposedly line out the golden rules for someone working with addicts. "Crisis Intervention" makes the list. You'd probably expect it to be number one on the list. Nope—it's number *eight*. Eight out of twelve. "Crisis Intervention" apparently is supposed to come *after* "Case Management," "Counseling," "Treatment Planning," "Assessment," "Orientation," "Intake," and "Screening."

I mean no offense to anyone, but when the hell is that supposed to be a workable plan for dealing with an addict? I'm dealing with an addict who was shooting smack just hours ago, or still has speed running through his body, and I'm supposed to walk through these other seven steps before treating things like a crisis?

Yeah right. And we wonder why the standard treatment industry fails 95% of the time.

---

[1] See John Herdman's book, Global Criteria: The 12 Core Functions of a Substance Abuse Counselor

Rehab starts at the crisis of withdrawal

When you're taking your first steps into sobriety, the junk is still in your system—and it will fight back. Intense, physical withdrawal periods are different from person to person and from addiction to addiction. But it is always harsh as hell.

For some addictions—specifically, alcohol and benzos—this withdrawal period itself can be life-threatening. Cutting your body off from the heroin or cocaine it has come to depend on will throw your body into serious shock.

Whatever your plan to be in or out of professional treatment, it's vital that you recognize the dangers of the withdrawal phase. If your addiction was to drugs or alcohol and you aren't in an actual inpatient care center, you need to at least be working with trained medical professionals in this period.

Even if you're addicted to a non-substance like gambling or sex, the withdrawal period will hit like a freight truck. You're still primed for all of the addiction habits you've been living, and those habits do not go lightly. There's a physical withdrawal component and an emotional withdrawal component to addiction, so it's like fighting a battle on two fronts.

Now I don't say this to scare you. I obviously don't say it to suggest that it's not worth the struggle—of course it is. But you need to go into these first steps with your eyes open to what's ahead, ready to fight the good fight.

It's also vital to note that treatment centers are there to ease the pain of withdrawal periods. It's still not going to be fun, but quality treatment will make it so much easier to get through. Sometimes that means medication to ease withdrawal symptoms, sometimes it just means a supportive and safe environment for you to be in.

But yes, even in the supportive environment of an inpatient center, withdrawal is never fun. If you're one of the millions of chronic relapsers, you've been here before. Withdrawal sucks, so what's say we make sobriety actually stick this time?

The only way out is through.

Compassion in the face of crisis

When someone walks into any treatment facility, they are still on a ledge. It doesn't matter if that person walked in themselves or if they arrived in handcuffs. The fact remains that this person is standing on a ledge at the top of a cliff thinking about what to do.

I want you to really pictures this. Close your eyes if it helps. Your son or daughter, friend, loved one, whoever it is to you, is walking into a treatment center after suffering out in the world for who knows how long. Suffering from suicidal depression, smoking crack, or slamming needles of heroin into their veins. Trying to numb the pain and quiet the torment in their head.

This person is suffering deeply, oftentimes barely lucid, and what's the standard response? Sign some paperwork, check them into a bed, and throw some books at them. Here's the *Big Book of Alcoholics Anonymous*. Here are *The 12 Steps and 12 Traditions*. Here's every piece of literature we have that will tell you about how messed up you are. Now, literally pick up this stack of books which feels like it weighs a thousand pounds, and go 'get started,' because we've got another addict to check in right behind you.

These people are human beings, confused and in pain, standing on a ledge on the verge of toppling over and dying. The solution is not to stack books on them. The solution is to meet them where they're at and compassionately coach them off that ledge and down to safety.

At this point, there's still first-aid care that needs to be given…and treatment centers these days are dropping the ball. I've gone toe-to-toe with clinical directors of facilities. I've seen people in detox who aren't getting the care they desperately need, and when I stand up for them I've been told, "You don't do it our way, so we are not going to refer anyone to you." Treatment is stuck in the past and seemingly content with a 95% failure rate.

We can do better than this.

The best thing I ever learned was that when a client walks into the room, the first thing I say is, "How can I help you?"

I'm not a twelve-stepper, and I'm not a non-twelve-stepper. It's totally irrelevant at the beginning of treatment. At the very first stages, addicts are not capable of even comprehending any of that stuff. Most of them—including myself at the time—are struggling to comprehend getting down from the ledge.

So, I make the radical decision to actually listen to what these people need. How about you let me take a nap and get some food, and then we can talk about the finer points of sobriety philosophy later? Deal.

My job is to make sure that each recovering addict wants to come back the next day. That's what I do when I treat people. I meet people where they are at each and every day. When they're ready to do a 12-step program—or a different recovery program—it's because *they* are ready for it. My goal is to make sure that clients are emotionally sober enough to make their own choice about what they should do, 12-step or not 12-step, with a clear mind. Clients need to be emotionally mature enough and sober enough to comprehend what the hell everyone's talking about. Otherwise, it's all lost.

When people are just beginning their treatment, they're not looking for long-term solutions to practice for the next five years, or even the next five weeks. They're struggling and looking for help to get through the next *day*. As caregivers, we need to understand this and really meet clients where they're at.

In the first stages of recovery, when withdrawal is rearing its ugly head and the addict is still teetering on a ledge, we as caregivers need to be in crisis mode. Not to pile books on them, but to respond to their needs, and help them get to a point where the real work of sober living can begin.

Chapter Nine
The Two Hidden Pitfalls Ahead of You

The first few weeks into sobriety are tough, but people tend to know that going in.

There's less common awareness about the relapse pitfalls further on down the road—and you only have to look at the rates of addiction relapse to see the evidence of that.

Whatever your addiction, there are some common points in the first few months of sobriety where relapses spike. When you know what's ahead of you, what to expect, and how best to deal with it, you're far more likely to charge through these times without falling off the rails.

When I was in treatment, I started noticing patterns of when fellow addicts seemed most likely to relapse and fall back into addiction. In my years working on the other side as an addiction caregiver, I've been able to see these danger zones even more clearly—and understand what's behind them.

The first hidden pitfall: "The Home-from-the-Honeymoon Crash" at 3-5 weeks

Withdrawal is a hellhole, and when you're first past it you're going to feel great. But here's a bitter irony—that honeymoon phase of sobriety can set you up for failure.

When you start to move past the withdrawal phase, your body and mind are on a huge upswing. If you were addicted to drugs or alcohol, the junk at this point is almost entirely out of your system. Your liver can start to breathe again, your brain isn't constantly being hammered with synthetic opioids, and your body is loving it.

Your mind is starting to clear again. You discover that, wow, it is actually possible to wake up in the morning (not afternoon) in a body that doesn't feel like shit, with a mind that isn't full of shame and regret. Birds seem more chipper, the sun seems even sunnier, and things are just dandy.

Odds are good that, at this point, you've been spending your recovery time in a treatment center. This artificial environment has been custom created to try to maximize your recovery potential. You've been removed from the dark chaos of your life before treatment.

In an ideal treatment world, this is where the real work begins. You're now stable and sober enough to begin the process of understanding the roots of your addiction and really changing your life from the ground up.

But, the standard treatment industry is far from ideal.

For way too many recovering addicts, this is the precise point at which their 30-day treatment runs out. And people feel so great, they don't think twice about happily checking out of treatment. They feel good right now, so they must be cured, right? The treatment worked, right? They're going to be lucky enough to be in that 5% that actually stays sober, right?

Wrong.

These recovering addicts feel great in that honeymoon afterglow after the first few weeks…and then they go back home.

They go back home to a life that's been ravaged by years of addiction. Back to unpaid bills, back to resentful family members, back to a social life dominated by addiction. Suddenly they're the only one of their friends that doesn't drink, shoot smack, gamble. Back to the normal stresses of life that everyone faces, but without their favorite way of coping with it.

This period is treacherous. Addicts suddenly swing from "I've got this" to "Holy crap I don't got this." The structures of their old lives pull them back towards their addiction, and their inability to deal with stress any other way makes it that much harder to avoid.

And again, this is the exact moment that most treatment programs are giving people a clear bill of health and sending them out the door. Pretty messed up, isn't it?

When the honeymoon starts to wane, that's when we've got to get to work on the deeper issues. Start actually building a sober life that works, and a sober mindset able to deal with real life.

This is why I always tell clients that if they're thinking they can just complete 30 days and be done with treatment, they're setting themselves up to fail. This point, three to five weeks in, is when we really get started.

The second hidden pitfall: "Hitting the Wall" at 7 to 9 weeks

This second hidden pitfall is even murkier and harder to see coming than the first.

Let me take you back to when it hit me.

At the time, I was maybe 60 or so days into treatment. I can't remember what I'd been doing that day, but it was something outdoors, and I'd been wearing flip flops in the mud. So here I am in the shower that evening, bent over and scrubbing my feet. After my feet are all squeaky clean, I stand up.

I know, this doesn't seem like a story about being on the brink of relapse, does it?

I stand up in the shower, and since I was bent over for a while, I get a head rush. This head rush just hits me hard, and suddenly I realize how much it feels like that first huge head rush from when I would take a big hit of crack cocaine. Bam, suddenly I'm hit by this insanely intense urge to smoke crack.

I just started bawling, right there in the shower.

See, I had been putting the work in. I was two months deep into treatment, and I was making a whole lot of progress. I was getting my life and head back together, and I felt like I was finally getting out of the woods. Like maybe I was going to beat this thing for good this time.

And then that craving hit, as strong as it ever was.

This is what I call "The Wall" danger zone. It hits when, like me, you've been putting in some serious work for a couple months. You've made progress, you've got a game-plan that you're executing every day, you're setting yourself up to win. Maybe you even get a little complacent, thinking it's all going to be smooth sailing from now on. Thinking you're just "over it."

But guess what? The cravings are still going to pop up, and you have to be ready for them, or they'll knock you right off your feet and put you back to square one.

Just because you've put a lot of hard work into losing 30 pounds doesn't mean you suddenly won't think cheeseburgers taste good or a huge bowl of ice cream wouldn't sound delicious. Just because an alcoholic is two months sober doesn't mean alcohol is suddenly going to taste terrible for the rest of time.

The will and desire to never revisit your addiction is wonderful and necessary—but it's just as important that you understand that the urges will come again. It seems a common pattern for this to knock people off their feet at roughly seven to nine weeks, but it's something to always remember—and be ready for.

> # When you can see the road ahead of you, you can steer clear of obstacles in your way.

A note on timing

No two people are exactly alike, and no two people will have the exact same recovery timeline.

I've given you here some rough time estimates for when these relapse pitfalls seem to be the greatest risk for most people, but the timing for you might not be the exact same. Just because you're at four weeks and one day doesn't mean you're free and clear from the home-from-the-honeymoon pitfall. If you leave a treatment center after six weeks, maybe it'll come at you then.

It's vital that you understand what's behind these danger zones—what causes them and how to be ready—so that you're prepared for them whenever they might pop up.

Chapter Ten
Defining Your Foundation

As your first 90 days in this journey of sobriety starts to wrap up, you'll find yourself looking at a massive transition—transitioning from inpatient care to outpatient care.

While you've been in an inpatient treatment center, literally everything around you has been designed with an intention to maximize your sober development. Each day has been structured, and the people around you aren't trying to sell you drugs or convince you to take "just one drink" to be social. You haven't had a landlord knocking down your door screaming about overdue rent, and you haven't been facing the day-to-day and hour-by-hour temptations of your old life.

When you move into this second 90-day quarter of sobriety, all that is about to change.

You're about to dive back into the 'real world' of your life outside of the artificial environment of inpatient care.

There are a few key strategies you can employ to make this transition as seamless and forward moving as possible. For obvious reasons, the transition from inpatient to outpatient care can be a really dangerous time for relapses. So, let's set you up to win instead.

Defining who you are—beyond addiction, beyond sobriety

In the 'old days' of your addiction, odds are your addiction pretty much defined you.

Serious drug addicts tend to not have a whole lot going on in their life outside of the addiction. They wake up each day either hurting from last night's binges or craving their next fix (or both). They scrounge up whatever money they can, with the single-minded intent of feeding that addiction. Their social circles are defined by the addiction, probably hanging out with other like-minded addicts. Or, their social lives are consumed by hiding the addiction as much as possible from everyone around them.

When you start living sober, suddenly all of that is (hopefully) out the window, behind you.

So, the question is, "Who are you now?"

How are you going to define yourself, think about yourself, and think about your life?

It might sound metaphysical or a little 'out there,' but this is a hugely important step—and one that often is overlooked.

When we don't have a clear sense of who we are and what defines us, we feel lost, aimless, floating through life, out of sorts, confused. All of this lends itself much more easily to addiction than sober living. If you don't have a clearly defined 'new' sense of self, addiction is going to pull you back in like gravity pulling you down, down, down.

A lot of addicts who come out of treatment start to define themselves entirely through their sobriety. Who am I? Well, I'm six months sober. What defines me? Um… not doing drugs. Being a recovering drug-addict.

Guess what—that sort of self-definition isn't exactly setting you up to win either.

For starters, you're still defining yourself in terms of the addiction. Plus, I bet you want more in life than just not doing drugs, or booze, or whatever.

So, the question is, how can you define yourself in such a way that *both* supports your sobriety *and* creates a strong sense of self above and beyond addiction?

Stop trying to find yourself, and start creating yourself.

Creating your foundation

The strategy you want to adopt here is creating your foundation: the three to five qualities or ideas that define the 'you' that you want to be.

These ideas and qualities will be ones that start to show up as you're doing work with your counselor. What sorts of things are important to you? How do you want to live your life? What mistakes have dragged you down in the past, and how can you flip them around to empower yourself?

This foundation that you're creating for yourself will play a pivotal role in connecting the work you do in developing sobriety to every other area of your life. You'll probably find that the ideas and qualities that really resonate with you stem in some way from your recovery work, but you'll also find them feeding directly into everything in your life. These will be the foundation of how you show up in your family, how you choose relationships and friendships, and how you move forward in your career. Like we've said before, sobriety is all about creating spiritual profitability—and this foundation is the bedrock on which you'll build that fulfilling life.

To give a clearer idea what this might exactly look like, I'm going to let you in on my personal foundation.

1. *I always choose myself first, no matter what.*

   You know those safety talks that airlines always give before a flight takes off? Remember the instructions for if the cabin loses pressure and oxygen masks fall down from above?

   "Always secure your mask first, before helping those next to you."

   This is the idea behind my first foundation—that I choose myself first.

   If this sounds selfish to you, you know what? It is. But there's 'good selfish' and 'bad selfish.' When I'm choosing to put myself first, I'm making the choice to create a better me, each and every day. And when I'm a better version of myself, I'm a better husband to my wife, a better brother or son or cousin to my family, a better counselor to my clients. By choosing myself first, I'm both helping myself and setting myself up to help others.

   It's the same logic behind those oxygen masks. The reason that they tell you to put your own on first is that if you try to help others first, you're probably just going to end up passing out. A parent might feel valiant trying to put their kid's mask on first, but what happens if they start getting dizzy and losing consciousness before they finish putting the mask on their panicking kid? Now neither parent nor child have their mask on. But, if the parent puts theirs on first, now they're stable and actually able to be there for their child.

That's a win-win. And that's how I live.

2. *I'm never afraid to shine a light on my weaknesses.*

I've got news for you—all of us have strengths, and all of us have weaknesses. Shocking, right?

I've got more news for you—real growth only happens when you're willing to face your weaknesses head-on and work on them.

It's easy and tempting for us to try to hide from or avoid our personal weaknesses. Heck, that probably played a big role in how your addiction started in the first place. But if you let yourself try to avoid your weaknesses and shortcomings, you're only hindering your own growth. It's like trying to drive forward with a flat tire, or with an engine firing on only half of its cylinders. You'll probably make some progress, but only a fraction of what's possible.

In my own life, I've seen clearly that when I shine a light on my weaknesses and look them straight in the face, that's when I grow the most. So, I'm committed to living that way each day.

3. *I'll never lower my expectations, always requiring others to rise to my level.*

I'm not going to sell myself out. Simple as that.

For people who are going to play a substantial role in my life—friends, business partners, family—I demand the same level of excellence that I demand of myself.

If you're an athlete who wants to really improve your game, you train with people better than you. If you're in business and you want to grow, you surround yourself with people even more knowledgeable and skilled than you are. Same idea in all areas of life. If you're going to play a more than casual role in my life, I'm going to demand greatness from you, just as I do myself.

4. *I always choose to fall forward.*

I've learned a deep, enlightening truth about myself: I am going to mess things up. A lot. And if you're a human being, guess what: you're going to mess things up too.

Everyone is going to trip and fall sometimes. If you expect otherwise, you're in for some rude awakenings. What really matters though, and what really determines your growth and development, is how you choose to look at and handle those mess-ups.

I always choose to fall forward.

I could look at my history of addiction as just total failure, but that would only hold me back. You know what? Being a full-blown, spoon-cooking crackhead made it possible for me to help thousands of people going through addiction. If I were focused on how I just totally screwed things up, I'd just be wallowing in self-pity and self-hatred. But that's not my style. When I fall forward, I learn from past mistakes, and turn them into just one more step towards greatness and growth.

A huge part of me finding my personal rhythm in this world is accepting that I'm just going to mess things up—and that's ok. Even falling is forward progress when you're committed to falling forward. Imagine a running back getting tackled at the one-yard line, throwing his body forward as he gets crunched to the ground, and barely making it into the end zone. It might not be pretty, but a touchdown is a touchdown.

Develop it now, hone it later

You'll want to start crafting this self-defining foundation towards the end of these first 90 days.

Thinking back on the metaphor of treating your life like a business—what sort of business do you want to be? What kind of products are you creating and selling? Who's your market, and who do you want to work with? What guiding ideas are going to make your business successful?

These are all questions that will begin to clarify your defining personal foundation. Write them down, chew on them, start living them, and as you move into the next 90 days, you'll find them taking on a more defined shape.

Then, you just keep on living them.

Chapter Eleven
Keep it Simple, Keep it Structured

Your next 90 days is all about keeping it simple. This is not the time to shake things up or make revolutionary life changes every day. This is not the time to jump headfirst into a new career or try out that wild new sleep schedule you read about online.

This is the time to live with routines, patterns, and structures.

When you were living as an addict, you were blowing with the wind. Finding drugs or booze whenever and however you could. Scrounging and hustling whatever money you could to feed that addiction, never knowing where your next dollar—or maybe even your next meal—would come from. Life was moment to moment, by the seat of your pants.

Guess what—that kind of erratic life gets to change now.

Especially as you first begin living outside of inpatient care, you get to surround yourself with structure, routine, and patterns. It's your fortress guarding against addiction.

This sort of structured routine means mapping out what you're going to be doing for pretty much every minute of the day. What time you wake up; when you eat meals; what times you're getting exercise, going to therapy, volunteering, or working at your job. Which days of the week you have which appointments. Even time to relax or unwind gets structured into your routine—maybe it's yoga each day from 4pm to 5pm, or playing pick-up basketball every Tuesday from 10am to 12pm.

The point is, you know ahead of time what you'll be doing on any given day, at any given hour.

I'm ten years out and still consider myself an outpatient, and you'd better believe my life is structured. I wake up at the same time every single day—weekdays, weekends, doesn't matter. I work out at the same time after waking up. Heck, I even eat pretty much the same meal every day, except for sometimes when I'm on vacation. If anyone ever hired a private investigator to track my movements, I'd be the easiest target imaginable. This structured life of routine and pattern has made my continued sobriety possible.

This also means that these first few months of outpatient life are *not* the time to take on any huge changes. The universe has a funny way of throwing you risks and temptations in this time, and they'll seem incredibly attractive. Maybe you get, out of the blue, an offer for some fantastic $300k-per-year job. Just a few months ago you were living in a van by the river, literally shitting in pizza boxes, and now these golden opportunities start flying at you.

It's not worth the risk.

Despite how amazing those opportunities sound, you've got to put your sobriety first. If you start jumping at huge new changes, you're putting your sobriety at risk. If the newly sober you is worth a $300k job offer today, you'll be worth a $300k job offer a few months or a year from now when you're more stable and able to make that change.

Keep it simple. Keep it structured. Keep it routine. Put your sobriety first now, and it will pay off down the line.

Always remember KISS: Keep It Simple, Stupid

Benefits of routine and structure

There are a whole ton of benefits to creating a structured, routine-based life when it comes to sustaining your sobriety. We're going to touch on just a few here, but this is far from a complete list.

1. *You're already experiencing huge change—structure helps avoid overwhelm.*

   Especially when you first begin your outpatient sober life, there's going to be a whole lot of changes in your life. New social circles, new ways of processing emotions, changes in your relationships, new perspectives on life.

   Creating a structured routine helps you create a solid foundation, a firm ground to stand on while all this change is happening around you. The more solid your day-to-day routine, the more equipped and able you'll be to navigate all the other changes in your life.

   This is hugely important in the work of developing your sobriety, but it holds true for any sort of big life changes you might make. Imagine you decide to make some big changes in your diet and exercise because you want to really start getting in shape and living healthy. Is it going to be best for you to just go to the gym whenever you feel like it and to try to come up with three healthy meal ideas every day?

Of course not.

If you're trying to adopt a new healthy lifestyle, structure is your friend there too. Schedule when exactly you're going to exercise ahead of time—maybe every morning at 7am, first thing in the morning. You'll also want to plan your meals ahead of time, so you know exactly what to expect. Maybe even prepare meals ahead of time, so they're ready to go.

If you play it loose and unstructured, it becomes so much harder to stick with big lifestyle changes, no matter what area of life. Structure makes change much easier, so set yourself up to win.

2. *Idle, unstructured time is your enemy. Boredom too.*

One of the most dangerous things for a recovering addict is a stretch of time when you don't have anything to do, you're feeling bored, and you've got no plans. That's the perfect opportunity for your addict-brain to start thinking about how great it would be to just have *one* little drink, or maybe call up your old drug-dealing friend—you know, just to see how he's doing.

They say idle hands are the devil's playthings. Well when it comes to addiction, idle time is addiction's playground. When you have every hour and every day mapped out ahead of time, you avoid these danger zones of boredom and unstructured risk.

3. *Structured routine helps you start building a stable life.*

When you were deep in the trenches of addiction, odds are you weren't exactly investing time and energy into the activities that make up a healthy, well-balanced life. Addicts aren't exactly role models for healthy diets, physical fitness, financial well-being, or anything else that makes up a stable life. When you're coming out of addiction, you don't have good habits in these areas.

Creating and living a structured plan helps make up for that lack of practice.

When you have a schedule for meals and exercise and work and therapy, you make it way more likely that you're actually going to do those things. And as you take care of yourself in these vital ways, you start to see the benefits. You start to build a healthy life—maybe for the first time in your life.

4. *Structure helps make sure you keep the sobriety work going.*

One of the most important parts of outpatient life is ensuring that you're keeping up with the work and growth of sober living.

As an inpatient, this was all pretty much unavoidable. You had a team around you making sure that you showed up for your counseling sessions or check-ins with doctors.

As an outpatient, it's just as important that you keep this momentum going—and creating a structured plan is the best path to success there. When you map out your hours and days, you'll know exactly when you're going to have your therapy and counseling sessions. You'll know when you're checking in at some sort of clinic or treatment center (which should be at least a few days every week). You'll know when you're meeting up with sober-living groups, like AA or NA meetings. By creating this routine pattern ahead of time, you're making sure that you keep on the rails with sober growth.

Again, this holds true for any area in your life where you're making big personal changes. If you're starting to take your personal health more seriously with diet and exercise, unstructured means uncommitted. If your plan is to go to the gym "whenever you feel like it," do you think you're going to be going as much as your body needs?

Yeah, probably not.

But if you plan out a structure ahead of time, let's say going to the gym five days a week, then it doesn't matter if some days you feel lazy. You've made a plan, and you stick with it. That's what makes serious personal growth possible.

Sober-living houses

A quick word on sober-living houses.

In short, unless you have a very safe, very predictable place to live, you should be staying in a sober-living home.

It's impossible to overstate how much your old life will try to suck you back into addiction. If you used to live in a drug-heavy neighborhood, or had roommates who drank or used drugs, going back to that same living situation is a huge risk...like, an incredibly huge risk...which you really should not take.

If you're not extremely confident in your living situation's ability to support your new sobriety, you should find a sober-living house to start your new outpatient life. Simple as that.

Your routine structure has already started

A lot of times I'll have clients come to me towards the end of their inpatient treatment, freaking out about not knowing how to start creating their new structured routine. And yeah, the idea of creating a pitch-perfect daily and weekly structure for your life can be intimidating, especially when for years past you've just been floating on the winds of addiction.

But guess what—at this point, you already have most of your structured routine ready to go. It's called inpatient treatment, and you've been doing it for weeks or months.

One of the biggest strengths of inpatient treatment is exactly this: that they create a structured, routine-heavy environment for you to live in. They do so for all of the reasons we've laid out in this chapter.

While you've been in inpatient treatment, you've been waking up and going to bed at the same time every day. You've been having your meals at the same time every day. You know exactly when you're going to have group counseling and when you're going to have individual counseling, when you're going to get some physical exercise, and when you're going to take some time to relax. Your every hour and minute has been structured in inpatient treatment.

So why feel like you need to start from scratch now that you're heading into outpatient treatment?

When you start planning the structure and routines for your life outside of inpatient treatment, make it easy on yourself. Start with the same structured routine you've been using already.

Your inpatient routine won't translate exactly one-to-one to your outpatient routine, but it will get you most of the way there.

When you're planning your outpatient routine, start with the routine you've already been living as an inpatient, and just swap out and change what needs to be changed. Instead of whatever physical exercise opportunities the treatment center has provided, schedule time to hit the gym or go to a yoga class. As soon as you have a job (and we'll discuss the importance of getting a job in a later chapter), plug in those work hours. Instead of inpatient counseling sessions, plug in your sessions with an outpatient therapist.

Basing your outpatient routine on your inpatient routine has the added benefit of making the transition that much more seamless. You've already been building habits of this routine, so continuing those habits is going to feel that much easier.

You're not alone, and you're not starting from scratch.

Chapter Twelve
Entering Your
Evolving Maintenance Mode

I've already said it before, and I'll say it again: even after over a decade of sobriety, I still consider myself an outpatient.

People tend to react with shock when they first hear this. "What???" they say. "Aren't you done with treatment yet? I mean, I get the whole 'an addict once is an addict forever' idea, but actually being in treatment for a decade sounds crazy."

But here's the thing. You probably own a car, right? A whole lot of time, effort, research, sweat, blood, and tears went into physically putting that car together. But does that mean once you buy a car, you never take it into a mechanic again?

No, of course not. If you want your car to actually last you awhile, you'll take it in for an oil change every few thousand miles. You'll have it fully inspected throughout its life. You'll be sure to top off fluids and replace parts as needed. The cars that have a nice, full life of 100,000 miles or more are the cars that were cared for throughout their life, the ones that were regularly taken in for maintenance.

What do you think happens if you never get your oil changed, and only bring your car to a mechanic after an accident or when the engine has completely crapped out on you? Well, you'll end up doing a lot of needless damage to your car. And you'll find out that, without regular maintenance, your engine is crapping out on you all the time and your car seems to always be in breakdown.

It's the same with pretty much everything in life. If you have a house and don't want it to fall into disrepair, it requires regular, ongoing maintenance.

Heck, same thing holds true in sports or in any other area of personal development. Do you think once athletes hit the pros, they're 'done' working out, practicing, or developing their skills? Of course not. They're always in maintenance and growth mode.

Sobriety is no different.

If you want to stay on this journey, you get to be in continuous maintenance mode. If you expect that at some point you should be 'done' with the work of sobriety, you're setting yourself up for failure—and relapse. Just like cars that aren't maintained, you'll find your 'sobriety engine' crapping out on you. And then right back into that relapse-rehab-repeat cycle.

So, let's break that cycle and start embracing this continuing maintenance mode instead, yeah?

Maintenance is continuous, but also evolving

Now, I may be in my second decade now of this ongoing, outpatient maintenance care, but that doesn't mean that my sobriety maintenance today looks the same as it did 10 years ago.

Just as each of us is growing and evolving, so will your outpatient care grow and evolve with you. As your relationship to sobriety grows, your needs will change as well. When I first left my last inpatient treatment center, I was checking with clinics, therapists, and counselors multiple times every week. These days, I meet with my various therapists and coaches maybe once a month. Not because I'm doing any less personal development now or am any less committed to my sobriety now, but simply because where I am now doesn't carry the same necessities.

Similarly, I'm not seeing the same specialists these days that I was ten years ago. The best therapists, coaches, and counselors are the ones with specialties. Some are highly trained for fresh-out-of-rehab counseling, others for years-down-the-line counseling.

Think about the teachers you've had. You may have had the world's best 1st-grade teacher, but would you want to still be learning from the same teacher in 9th grade? Of course not. Not because that teacher was any less effective eight years later, but because their specialty just no longer fit your needs.

The ongoing work of sobriety is just the same. What it looks like for you exactly is going to evolve and change, as your needs evolve and change. But staying in the game, staying committed, is the one constant to stick to.

> # When you're developing sobriety, you're building spiritual profitability. When you're spiritually profitable, your life becomes golden.

'Sobriety maintenance' has some great side effects

So, here's the thing.

When I start talking about this with addicts, especially those just getting ready to leave inpatient treatment centers, sometimes all they can hear is, "This work is just going to take over the rest of my life." And when I talk about this with the family members of addicts, sometimes all they hear is, "My son or daughter is never going to finally be well again."

Folks, this is missing the big picture here.

Like we've talked about already, sobriety is all about becoming spiritually profitable—accepting who you are, loving yourself, finding your rhythm and purpose in the world, creating a life you can be proud of, et cetera.

'Sobriety maintenance' is all about continuing this growth, continuing to look at your shortcomings and developing them into strengths, continuing to take on your bad habits and transform them into empowering ones, continuing to grow, to bettering your relationships, to becoming more and more the person you want to be.

Guys—all of this is about way more than making sure you keep away from drugs and booze. It's about creating the life that you want.

I look back on my addiction, and you know what? I'm grateful for it. I'm grateful that I went way down that rabbit hole and became a full-fledged, spoon-cooking crackhead. No joke.

Because if I hadn't become such an addicted mess, I wouldn't have done all of the work and all of the personal growth that I have over these years. I wouldn't be as spiritually profitable as I am today if it weren't for the addiction that first put me on this path.

I'm married to a brilliant, beautiful woman, the girl of my dreams. I know that all of the work I've put into myself these last years is what makes that relationship possible.

This isn't just some chore you're burdened with. This isn't some hassle that you have to slog through for however long you want to stay sober. This is the path to a brilliant, growing, spiritually profitable life.

Embrace it. Savor it. Have fun with it (yes, it can be fun). There'll be ups and downs, times where it feels easy and times where it challenges you; but it's all worth it. Believe me, because I've been down this same road, my friend.

Chapter Thirteen
Breaking Down Sobriety: Physical vs. Emotional

We tend to think of sobriety in pretty simple terms. "Sobriety" to most of us just means 'not doing *that*,' right? As in, not drinking, not doing drugs, not gambling, or not doing whatever your addiction was.

Wrong. If that's all that sobriety means to you, get ready to relapse, Bud. Trust me, I've been there. Way too many times actually.

If you want to really be on this lifelong journey of sobriety and not just a relapse-rehab yo-yo for the rest of your life, sobriety has got to mean more than just 'don't do that thing you used to do.'

Two sides of a coin

Sobriety can be thought about in two categories.

First, we've got *physical sobriety*. This is pretty close to what most people think of when they think sobriety. If alcohol is your addiction, then physical sobriety means first and foremost: not drinking. Not drinking, not having any alcohol in your body from last night, and perhaps most importantly—keeping that up consistently for a continuous stretch of time. If you're 'sober' for nine days out of ten but blacking out every tenth, that sure doesn't make you 90% sober. That makes you a drunk with a schedule.

But again, physical sobriety is just one part of sobriety. After all, you could commit yourself to a personal jail and be locked in a cell 24/7 without any access to booze. But if you still thought about booze all the time, wished that you could grab a bottle to drown every problem, and begged anyone within earshot for just one little sip—is that really sobriety?

Obviously not. So, there's more going on here.

The second, lesser recognized, part of sobriety is *emotional sobriety*.

Emotional sobriety can be summed up as the ability to get in touch with one's emotions and, more important, to allow oneself to feel those emotions organically and naturally.

I know, I hear you groaning already.

Addicts don't like this because the goal is always to numb out or avoid. Kill the emotions, kill the pain, stop feeling, or flood the brain with dopamine and create a forced feeling of temporary pleasure. That's the ticket.

If there's any presence of an emotion—especially a tough emotion— the response from an addict is to indulge in their drug of choice to kill it. Food, heroin, cocaine, alcohol, gambling…pick your poison. Maybe it's a co-dependent relationship or sexual partner that helps wipe your emotional slate blissfully clean and escape the reality of the day.

Let's be clear though: addiction isn't just about artificially avoiding or replacing unpleasant emotions. Addiction can also very much be about hyper-exaggerating your already pleasurable emotions.

When I was an addict, being just 'happy' was never good enough for me. I couldn't be having a 'good time' at a party. I had to be having an insane, over-the-top, heart-racing, *amazing* time. It wasn't good enough for me to just be dancing. Heck, it wasn't good enough for me to be dancing on top of the bar. I had to be dancing on top of the bar completely trashed, wearing a grass skirt and nothing underneath.

I had to always be happier-er-er. 'Happy' wasn't good enough, and 'happier' wasn't good enough—I had to throw on a few extra "ers."

This emotional self-manipulation is the real core of addiction. And so emotional sobriety is the real core of sobriety. Throughout my own journey, it quickly became very clear to me that physical sobriety alone does not mean shit. It just doesn't.

Simple abstinence won't get you where you want to be. Changing your beliefs, desires, attitudes, and thinking will create the life you want.

No one wants to be a dry drunk

Have you ever heard the term 'dry drunk'? That is exactly what I didn't want to be: sober and pissed off. Sober and unable to deal with life, unable to deal with myself and my emotions.

At first, at the slightest provocation, I'd be saying to myself, "This sucks. I'm so pissed off all the time. I can't talk to that girl. Can't do it. No way. I need an eight ball in my pocket. I need a pack of Parliament cigarettes. And actually, I might need a second eight ball for my other pocket. Without all that, no way can I talk to these girls. Or deal with people. Or deal with freaking anything."

Yeah let's be real, that's not exactly sober thinking, is it?

That line of thinking is born out of the fear that without all those things I will be *exposed*. People will see the real me. For an addict, that can be way too much a risk and an impossible burden to bear.

My goal became *not* to get *x* number of days physically sober.

My goal became to master my thoughts, because I had a serious thinking problem. A serious emotional problem. A serious 'dealing with life' problem.

Chapter Fourteen
Building Your
Emotional Sobriety

In my work as an addiction counselor, I've noticed a trend of sorts. Clients will come into my office all pumped up, huge smile on their face, and they'll happily tell me, "Ross, I just hit 30 days sober. I've got no cravings or urges to use, and it's freaking great."

I always have a nervous chuckle.

I say, "I'm really psyched that you have 30 days sober under your belt, but to be honest it doesn't really mean shit—yet. Because emotions are going to come at you out of nowhere. Someone's going to give you the finger on the way to work. Or your husband is going to be a real jerk one morning.

"Or you know what? Sometimes life is just going to get real rough. People lose jobs. Heck, someone you love is going to die at some point."

Thirty days sober is great, but the real key to long-term, life-long sobriety is being able to maintain that sobriety when life falls off the rails. And the key to *that* is emotional sobriety.

Experiencing life, accepting your emotions

Emotional sobriety is all about having organic feelings and emotions, and dealing with them.

People can get addicted to a whole range of things, but at the end of the day pretty much every addiction serves one core purpose for the addict: artificial emotional control.

Have a shitty day, and now you're feeling like crap? Drink to numb the pain. Feeling stressed by your job and your marriage? Hit the casino for that sweet rush when you win, and the lights and bells go off. Feeling anxious and desperate to relax? Smoke a fat joint and melt into the couch.

When we're addicted to something, we're really addicted to being able to artificially change how we feel. And if you want to beat addiction, you need to start being able to feel those feelings. The good and the bad.

Life is a roller coaster, and emotional sobriety means accepting the ride—the fun parts, the scary parts, the sad parts, the happy parts, the whole package.

My mom died a couple years ago. She was 82 years old and died totally unexpectedly. She was watching a movie in the theater with her boyfriend, and as the credits started rolling, she stood up, walked up the aisle, and died right there. Just fell over and died.

I remember getting a call from the police department back home telling me that I needed to call the emergency room. I made the call, and the nurse there simply said, "I regret to inform you that your mother has passed away."

I felt absolutely shattered.

When I was in treatment, we'd all write lists of triggers—things that we thought might set us off emotionally and make us spin out of control and go back to drugs. Every time I wrote one of those lists, one future event was always at the top: my mother's death.

After the funeral, I flew back home by myself. My wife, Meg, had gone home before me, and I arrived to a dinner with one of my in-laws and a childhood friend. It's about six o'clock in the evening, getting dark outside. I'm looking out of a window, when a monarch butterfly suddenly lands on the sill.

Meg mouths to me, "That's your mom."

I'd already cried so much at this point, but looking at that butterfly, I just got up and casually went to the bathroom and started quietly weeping again.

That butterfly didn't leave the window for the entire night. In the morning when I got up, it was still there. I walked outside, said hello to it, and it jumped up and flew off.

I honestly feel like my mom was there as that butterfly, waiting to go to the "other side" until she knew that I was ok. The memory brings such a sense of peace and love still to this day.

I had predicted that my mother's death would be a huge trigger for me, and you know what? It was rough. Horrible at times. If I hadn't put so much time and energy into building my emotional sobriety, I would have lost it. Would have gone back to my addiction to avoid the emotions. But because I didn't, I was able to fully experience the experience. Including that beautiful moment, my final connection with my mom that has become one of my most treasured memories.

That's the thing about life. If you try to control your emotions, you only end up missing out. If I'd descended back into drugs when my mom died, I would have never had the chance to see her as that monarch butterfly and watch her fly off to whatever's next.

Your addiction might feel like the easy solution to life's emotional problems, but I can guarantee you that you're only robbing yourself of the real magic.

Emotional sobriety goes beyond your addiction

I once worked with a favorite client of mine, a woman who had a serious vodka addiction.

Post-traumatic stress or post dramatic growth. You choose.

She told me how she had a ritual that was dear to her. Every day, she would go out onto her balcony to enjoy the sunset. Her house had a gorgeous view. From her balcony, she would look out over Pebble Beach golf course, and past that out towards the Pacific Ocean. You can imagine how incredible those sunsets were. Whenever this woman would sit in front of this breathtaking view, she'd be enjoying a nice glass of chardonnay.

In treatment, she told me flat out, "Look, I know I have a vodka problem, and I want to stop that. But I'm never giving up my one glass of chardonnay while watching the sunset."

She was so stubborn on this point, and one day I just said to her, "So let me get this straight. You're sitting on your balcony, overlooking this incredible vista, watching this mind-boggling ball of fire sink below the horizon. Half the time you're seeing dolphins or whales playing out in the ocean. And you think the glass of wine is what makes it so special? You just *have* to have the wine with it—otherwise it's not good enough for you?"

Emotional sobriety is about feeling your emotions and experiences authentically and with a sober mind. If you mess around with something that messes with your emotions, you're playing with fire.

I get the question a lot about whether marijuana is addictive or not. If someone is in treatment for their addiction to opiates, do they have to stop smoking weed too?

In my own case, I would ask myself, "I know I have a cocaine problem, but do I have a drinking problem?"

I'll be honest with you. I don't think I have an alcohol problem. I don't. But I haven't had a drink in over 10 years. Why? Because if you're sitting at the bar having a drink or two, at some point you're going to get a little buzz. And when you get a buzz, maybe that person across the bar suddenly looks more attractive. Well guess what? That buzz can make an eight ball start to look more attractive too.

Things that influence your emotions influence your emotions. Simple as that. A beer or two might not ruin my life, but it's just grease on a slippery slope right back to cooking crack in my kitchen, spending thousands every day on cocaine. So why even play with that?

You want to relax? I get it, so do I. But you really can't relax without smoking a joint? You really need that artificial aid? People in our culture have become so conditioned to looking for that quick fix, that magic pill that will make them lose 20 pounds, or that get-rich-quick scheme that will make them a millionaire overnight. But we all know that if it sounds too good to be true, it probably is.

If you're serious about sobriety, if you are *really* committed to ending the relapse cycle, emotional sobriety needs to become your best friend. And if you're using an artificial crutch to deal with your feelings and emotions—even if that crutch wasn't your main addiction—then you're not living emotionally sober. And you're setting yourself up for failure.

But on the flipside, if you really commit to emotional sobriety, then you'll finally be able to break that cycle of relapse. And then you'll really start experiencing the magic of life.

PART TWO

Lifelong Relapse Prevention

Chapter Fifteen
Understanding Relapse

Creating sustainable sobriety is, at its core, a journey on two fronts: on one side, continuing your inner work of emotional sobriety and spiritual profitability, and on the other side, practicing relapse prevention.

Now, these two fronts have distinct qualities, but they're also intertwined and mutually supportive. The work of developing your emotional sobriety and nurturing your spiritual profitability is itself going to decrease the dangers of relapse. At the same time, the work that goes into preventing relapses also bolsters your emotional sobriety and spiritual profitability. The two go hand in hand, each building and supporting the other.

We've already discussed emotional sobriety and spiritual profitability, and we'll continue to develop your understanding and strengths there. But in much of this second section of this book, we're going to focus more on relapse prevention.

To lay the foundations for relapse prevention, let's first clarify what exactly we're talking about.

Relapse is a return to indulging your addiction—and addictive thoughts

Just as physical sobriety is essentially "not doing that thing you were addicted to," relapse is essentially "doing that thing again." Relapse is the sneaky, slippery, heartbreaking demon of addiction.

I'll be blunt—if you're given the standard resources, it's not that hard to get sober. I know that might sound ridiculous, but stick with me.

If you have the means to get yourself into an inpatient treatment program, you're probably going to get sober at least for the time that you're there. Even if it's the typical 30-day program which sends you out the door before you're ready and doesn't give you the personal, one-on-one attention that you need while you're there, you're still probably going to 'get sober' in those 30 days.

The problem isn't this short-term *getting* sober. The problem is *staying* sober.

Remember, the addiction treatment industry today has a 95% failure rate. But that doesn't mean 95% of people who enter into treatment bail before completing their inpatient stay. And it sure doesn't mean that 95% of those people are still doing drugs while in those treatment centers. That 95% failure rate is made up mostly of people who 'get sober' for a period of time, but then fall right back into their addiction.

For a long time, I was one of those statistics. I'd go to a rehab program and clear the junk out of my system for a while. But it was only a matter of time before addiction pulled me right back in. Then back to rehab at some point, then relapsing again at some point, then back to rehab, and on and on and on.

This rehab-relapse cycle claims millions of addicts. People bounce back and forth, never truly getting a grip on sustainable sobriety, until they eventually overdose and die, or their life just completely falls apart and they end up on the streets.

This is the elephant in the room, the tragic failure of the treatment industry as it exists today. But it's a failure that can be fixed. With the team of experts I work with, we're doing our damnedest to spread solutions.

And that's all about lifelong relapse prevention.

> # "Just 'cause you got the monkey off your back doesn't mean the circus has left town."
>
> ## - George Carlin

Relapse is a three-step cycle

People often think of a relapse as an instantaneous event—that moment when the booze touches your lips and your days-sober counter hits zero again, or the instant you start sniffing up another line of coke.

But guess what—moments like that don't just happen spontaneously, out of the blue. I can pretty much guarantee that you're never going to be just walking down the street, happily sober as can be, then suddenly trip and fall onto a loaded needle of heroin. You're not going to just fall into a vat of beer.

Relapse isn't a spontaneous event. It's a downward slope towards using again, and it's a slope that has three sections.

1. Emotional relapse

Any relapse always starts with an emotion.

Let me repeat that, just so everyone is clear: relapse always starts with an emotion.

This is one of the things that most treatment programs whiff on. They don't talk about emotional relapse, they talk about physical relapse—and assume that physical relapse is just caused by a physical place. They'll talk about how you should avoid bars or hanging out with your old drug dealer, but they'll pretty much never talk about your emotions.

Now you might be saying, "But wait, Ross! In those chapters about emotional sobriety, you kept telling me that I had to start experiencing my natural emotions, not trying to avoid painful emotions or amp up pleasurable emotions. You told me to feel those emotions organically, but now you're saying emotions are the start of relapses? What the heck, man?"

All good points, dear reader. Here's the difference: relapses start when an emotion *gets the better of you.*

There's a big difference between experiencing an emotion and letting an emotion get the better of you. So, what does it mean for an emotion to get the better of you?

Emotions get the better of you when they overwhelm you, when they become your entire world, and you find yourself unable to still be in the driver's seat of your life.

As an analogy, imagine someone dealing with their 15 minutes of fame. Especially in this age of the internet, it seems like everyone really does get their 15 minutes of viral fame.

Maybe someone slipped and fell while walking down the aisle at their wedding, and then kept slipping and tripping while trying to stand up. Someone was taking video of it, the video gets on the internet, and before you know it, it's going viral. It's racking up millions of views on YouTube, people are putting goofy music in the background to make it even funnier, the whole nine yards.

Now, even with a grounded, emotionally stable response, that's going to suck. That person is probably going to feel embarrassed and awkward about the situation. But nothing is popular for long on the internet, and it won't be long until those 15 minutes of fame are up, and everyone else starts to forget.

If our hero here has a solid grip on their emotions, they start to move past it too. The embarrassment fades, and they move on with their life. Emotions come, and emotions go.

But if the emotions here are getting the better of them, they just can't let it go. Every morning, they're still waking up mortified. Their friends and family are saying it's not such a big deal, but they just can't let it go. Everyone else is forgetting it and moving on, except for the person who's overwhelmed and taken over by their emotions.

Remember, pleasurable emotions can get the better of you too. Maybe someone hit their 15 minutes of fame because they were a one-hit wonder on YouTube with a music video that briefly went viral and became hugely popular. In this example, an emotionally grounded person would enjoy the ride while it lasted, then move forward afterwards. But someone who gets overwhelmed by the experience will keep trying to milk it out, trying to stretch those 15 minutes of fame into a lifetime. Always talking about it, thinking about it, trying to rekindle the magic, trying to create a career all around playing that one briefly viral hit of theirs. They can't deal with and process the experience, and they can't move forward through it. They get stuck.

When an emotion gets the better of a recovering addict, it triggers the thought—whether conscious or unconscious—of "Shit, I cannot deal with this."

Which leads right to the next part of relapse.

2. Mental relapse

Mental relapse is when that overwhelming emotion leads into addicted thoughts.

Maybe you'll start thinking about how easy it would be for you to get a grip on your out-of-control emotions with just one small drink. Maybe you start thinking back on your days in the trenches of addiction, remembering all the fun times and ignoring all the awful consequences. Maybe you start rationalizing to yourself some bullshit about how you've 'earned' just one little indulgence, or how no one else needs to know, or how you've got control of it now and can handle just a little bit.

Human beings are, for better or worse, really good at bullshitting themselves. Mental relapse is all about that little bullshit artist in your head. Rationalizing, justifying, twisting, and manipulating your memories. Mental relapse can include all of that and more.

And when mental relapse spirals out of control, it leads to the final end-point of the relapse slope.

3. Physical relapse

Physical relapse is when you start taking actions that lead back to your addiction. Physical relapse is when you call up your old dealer and set up a time and place to buy, or when you drive to the liquor store and grab a bottle, or when you go into a casino and sit down at your favorite slot machine again.

Physical relapse reaches its fateful conclusion when you take that sip of booze, or light up that first hit, or pull that first slot lever, or indulge again in whatever your personal addiction was. And you dive back into the muddy trenches of addiction.

Relapse prevention is about preventing and interrupting that cycle

Relapse is insidious. For a lot of addicts, they don't even see it coming. Suddenly they find themselves using again, and sobriety seems hopeless.

But don't worry—there is a way out.

When you understand how relapse works, and when you're equipped with tools and strategies to prevent and interrupt the relapse cycle, you won't be caught off guard. You'll be armed with the capability to avoid relapse today, tomorrow, and the next day.

And day by day, quarter by quarter, you'll stay sober—and build the life that you want.

Chapter Sixteen
Identifying Emotional Triggers

Every time I went into a treatment center, there were some slight variations in how treatment was presented and the work that we as patients did. But despite those variations, there were some common practices that showed up every time.

One of those exercises that every treatment center had addicts do, without fail, was to come up with a list of triggers.

Even if you're only slightly familiar with addiction treatment, you're probably aware of the concept of triggers. It's one of those treatment practices that has bled out into the cultural awareness as a whole.

The idea of triggers is that there are certain things that will shove a recovering addict towards relapse.

Relapse is the three-step cycle of emotional relapse, mental relapse, and physical relapse which we discussed in the last chapter. A trigger is the starting point that first activates that cycle.

And just like we talked about in the last chapter, despite the reality that relapse really starts with an emotion, these treatment centers all acted like relapse was just a physical action that was triggered by a physical thing.

Every time I was in treatment, I'd find myself writing out a list of what I thought would be triggers for me. The triggers we were told to list would always be things outside of ourselves. Places that we might find ourselves that would crank up a sudden urge to relapse and start doing drugs again. People in our lives that would trigger an urge to relapse. Things in our life that might drop us into a relapse spiral. Events that could launch us back into addiction. The triggers we talked about were always external like that. People, places, things, events. Listing out these external triggers, over and over again. These triggers were drilled into our heads.

So many times, I'd come out of a treatment program and basically turn myself into a shut-in. I figured if I just physically avoided all of those triggers, I'd have to be fine, right?

I literally would not leave my apartment for a solid month. I'd make it physically impossible for me to encounter any of those triggers that I'd listed out. If I didn't leave my apartment, I couldn't find myself in any of those 'danger' places. If I didn't let anyone in, I would never encounter those 'dangerous' people. Problem solved, right?

Obviously not. If that strategy worked, I wouldn't have relapsed as many times as I have.

Even when I went into hermit mode, I was still dealing with cravings and urges. I'd still have days when the temptation was wild and days when I felt like I had a grip on sobriety.

So, if I was still avoiding these 'thing' triggers, but was still *feeling* triggered towards relapse, what the heck was going on?

> # When you know your emotional triggers, you know your route to success.

Triggers aren't about the things—they're about emotions

Here's the thing, folks. Triggers aren't really about these physical 'things' that every standard treatment program has you list out. Triggers are all about emotions. This is why the first step of the relapse cycle is 'emotional relapse.'

Even if you go to a bar the night you get out of an inpatient center to hang out with friends, you're not going to physically fall into a vat of beer or slip into a kiddie pool filled with vodka.

Even if you go to a wild party with your old drug-using friends, you're not going to literally trip into a pile of cocaine. I've been to a lot of drug-fueled parties, and I can tell you that I have never physically fallen into a pile of cocaine.

Even if you go to your old drug dealer's house just to say hello, he's almost certainly not going to sneak up behind you and jab a needle of heroin into your arm.

So, what's really the deal with triggers?

Triggers are all about circumstances that make it *more likely* for your emotions to get out of balance. The 'trigger' that truly launches you into a relapse danger zone is an emotional trigger—a moment when your emotions get the better of you.

Every time I wrote one of those 'trigger lists' in a treatment center, the #1 potential trigger I'd list was the death of my mother. Out of everything I could imagine, all the places I could go, people I could be with, things I'd encounter, or events to happen to me, my mother's future death always stood out to me as the most likely to send me spiraling back into drugs or alcohol.

Looking on that with the understanding of emotional sobriety, the reason for that is pretty clear. Again, the danger wasn't that I'd inherit a suitcase of 8-balls, or that there would be piles of cocaine scattered around the funeral. Obviously, it was not a literal, physical danger of a relapse just jumping into my face unexpectedly.

No, the death of my mother was my #1 trigger because I knew that it would be emotionally devastating, and would represent a huge risk to my emotional stability and emotional sobriety. If the emotions became so overwhelming that I didn't know how to deal with them, I knew that I had a go-to way to deal with that: a whole lot of drugs.

Well, as I've already discussed, my mom did die. And it wasn't even the sort of passing that family and friends can prepare for, the quiet passing in a hospital where you have time to say final goodbyes. No, my mom passed away completely out of the blue. Talk about an emotional shock.

But did I relapse? No.

The emotions were no less devastating than I could have predicted back in those treatment programs. There were intense waves of grief, pain, sorrow, loss. Anyone who's lost a parent probably knows exactly what I'm talking about.

The loss of my mother didn't send me spiraling into relapse not because it wasn't emotionally painful, but because I had learned how to live with my emotions organically. How to feel what I was feeling naturally, accept it, and move forward through it. In short, I had years of emotional sobriety practice under my belt.

The real key to not letting triggers set you off is just that—emotional sobriety.

Uncovering your real triggers

Simply understanding that the real trigger dangers are overwhelming emotions is valuable. But even more valuable will be the process of uncovering precisely which emotions have a tendency to get the better of you, and beginning to learn how situations and circumstances—the 'things' of most trigger lists—can send you into that unstable emotional state.

You've probably created a trigger list at some point, and you can use that list to identify the emotions that present a danger to relapse.

To do so, the key is to take a superficial 'thing' trigger, and visualize a scenario in which that would lead to a relapse. Really play the situation out in your head. As you do so, the key question to ask yourself is: what emotion is getting the best of me in this scenario and leading to relapse?

Let me play out an example.

For me, one place that always made my 'things' trigger lists would be sports events. Back in the day, I used to love going to football games. The thrill, the excitement, the tension—I loved it. And every time I went to a game, I would get completely wasted...probably drunk by the time I got to the stadium, and progressively drunker as the game went on.

I could see that going to a football game would be a relapse danger for me, but the treatment programs I went to never helped me see *why*. So, let's play out the scenario.

Ok, say I'm going to a football game with the intention of staying sober. I get to my seat and the game is starting. Everyone around me is getting rowdier and rowdier, beer cups in hand. One thing I imagine here is feeling excitement during the game—but remember, I had to always be happier-er-er. So, I'm feeling excited, but it doesn't feel excited *enough*. Now I'm feeling the urge to drink so that I can crank my excitement up to the insane levels I'm used to. In this scenario, 'excitement' is the emotional trigger at play.

With this understanding, not only do I know that football games are a dangerous environment for me, but I also understand the emotional reason *why*.

And when you start really getting a handle on the *why*, you're better able to see dangerous emotional situations ahead of time, as well as continue building your emotional sobriety.

Chapter Seventeen
Strategic Planning –
How to Navigate Triggers

So, let's recap where we are at this point.

We know that the key to relapse, that first fateful step back into your addiction and addictive mental patterns, is an emotional state getting the better of you—whether that means you're overwhelmed by a painful emotion like anxiety, or you're overwhelmed by a pleasurable emotion like the urge to be happier-er-er-er.

You've begun identifying circumstances and situations that have a high risk of triggering this unstable emotional reaction, and you know that it's the emotional content of these things, not the things themselves, that are dangerous to your sobriety and stability.

So, what do you do now?

The goal is obviously not to take that list of emotional triggers and forever avoid anything that today seems like it could be a risk of stirring them up. As you practice emotional sobriety— living with your emotions organically—your ability to handle these situations will strengthen.

So how do you know when it's 'safe' for you to go to a football game, a family Christmas party, or a friend's wedding where you know there will be an open bar and rowdy crowd?

This is where *strategic planning* comes in.

Remember—these are life skills, not just addiction skills

It's worth remembering here that the skills and strategies I'm laying out for you are not just about navigating addiction. When we talk about ways to work past your addiction habits, we're really talking about ways to live a spiritually profitable life. These strategies and practices are valuable in any scenario where you're trying to build a better life or make new lifestyle changes.

Trying to lose weight, build better spending habits, get a handle on your anger, or any other big life changes? These strategic planning steps will make that progress possible.

This practice of strategic planning is one of the most valuable tools that anyone can adopt—addict or not. When you live your life with strategic planning, sure, you'll still meet unexpected obstacles. Life is chaotic and unpredictable.

But the idea with strategic planning is not that you'll know exactly how any situation is going to play out. The idea is that you'll be prepared to handle whatever comes your way. And you'll know ahead of time if a certain situation has risks that you *wouldn't* be able to handle—and you can steer clear of those situations accordingly.

> # "What got you here won't get you there."
> ## - Marshall Goldsmith

The steps of strategic planning

These are the steps you'll want to take before engaging any potentially risky situation. Some will sound familiar, as they're closely tied to how you identify your emotional triggers in the first place.

The more you practice this strategic planning, the more it will become second nature to you. So, let's dive right in:

1. Get clear on what the situation is

The first step is to be clear on what exactly you're considering. Clarity here is vital. The more clearly defined the situation, the more you can accurately plan ahead for all contingencies.

"Being around my family that likes to drink" might be a risky situation, but let's get more specific than that. A family event like going out to dinner at a classy restaurant is way different than a family reunion barbeque in Uncle Joe's backyard. A weeklong camping trip with your family is way different than a graduation party for your younger sibling.

Define the situation, and be specific.

As an example in this chapter, let's imagine that the situation your defining is "Going to a family wedding, the marriage of my cousin Sally and her fiancée Ted."

2. What are your motivations for going?

The next step is to ask yourself—why do you want to go?

Understanding your motivation is vital if you want to predict how you're most likely to respond in these situations. Do you want to go to Sally and Ted's wedding because you feel obligated to, and you know your family will give you crap if you don't? Do you want to go because Sally is one of your closest friends and you're super excited to celebrate her special day? Do you want to go because you know it's going to be a really fun party, and you miss hitting the dance floor? Do you want to go because you're hoping to meet someone to hook up with?

For any possible situation that you want to engage in, there are a million different possible motivations that you could be dealing with. And it's entirely possible that you'll have a mix of a few different motivations, some stronger than others.

Sometimes, just clarifying your motivations will activate some flashing-red warning sirens. If you're being honest with yourself and your main motivation for going to Sally's wedding is that there's an open bar and you're remembering how much fun you've had hanging out with drunk party-goers, maybe you'd better take a pass here.

3. What's probably going to happen around you?

The next step is to visualize what's going to be happening around you—and really walk through the whole thing in your mind.

What kind of atmosphere do you expect at Sally and Ted's wedding? Is it going to be a pretty relaxed event filled mostly with people just talking and laughing at dinner tables? Or is the main event going to be a rocking dance floor with strobe lights and fog machines and the whole nine yards?

Will people be drinking around you? If so, will the crowd be the 'one or two drinks to loosen up' type of crowd, or the 'let's get wasted and go crazy' kind of crowd?

Who else do you know will be there, and how are they probably going to interact with you? Does your family understand what you're going through, and know not to try to shove drinks in your hand? Is that one rowdy friend going to be there who's always trying to get you to take shots with him?

It's important here to imagine a variety of possibilities. The more you walk through what could possibly happen ahead of time, the less likely it is that you'll be caught off guard.

4. *When you're there, what emotions will probably come up?*

This step is where you really start to explore what your emotions are going to be in this situation—and whether or not you'll be able to stay in the driver's seat.

It's important here to not just assume that your emotions will match the general emotions of the event. Weddings are happy events, so you'll just be happy, right?

Well—maybe not.

If everyone around you is drinking, maybe you'll start to feel sorry for yourself, pitying yourself for having to be sober while everyone around you gets sloshed. Or maybe you'll get frustrated and angry at your family if they go wild with the booze, knowing how sensitive an issue it is for you. Or maybe you will feel happy—but then get overwhelmed by that urge to be *really, really* happy, the kind of happy where you have to be dancing on top of the bar with a lampshade on your head.

As you're walking through the possible emotions you'll experience, this is where you also want to be watching for red flags. Are the emotions you're anticipating the same emotions that tend to trigger you? When you're imagining the situation and your emotional response, does it seem like the emotions might be strong enough to get the better of you?

If so, your emotional sobriety might not yet be strong enough for you to safely jump into the situation.

5. *Who will be 'on your team' there?*

The next step is to look at who will be there with you, and more specifically, who will be there *for* you.

Will there be someone there that you know you'll be able to safely hang out with and talk to if things start to get crazy around you? Will there be someone there who understands what you're going through, and who is also committed to your sobriety?

Or will you be the only sober one there?

It's not necessarily a make-or-break deal for you to have a 'teammate' there with you. But it is important to know going in whether or not there's at least one person around you who you can go to if you need support. If it's just going to be you on your own, it means you have to be that much more secure and grounded in your emotional sobriety.

6. *What happens if things go south?*

This is one of the most important steps in the planning process—what happens if things go south?

Look, we all like to plan ahead, imagining that things are going to go great. It's a whole lot less fun to plan for the worst-case scenario. But if you're not clear on what that worst-case scenario is, and if you're not confident that you can handle it, then what do you think is going to happen if the worst-case scenario *does* arrive?

In our imaginary wedding example, what if everyone around you is just getting completely sloshed, and people start badgering you to drink with them? Or what if your parents launch into one of their alcohol-fueled screaming arguments? Maybe your ex is a friend of the couple—what if he or she starts flirting with you again?

And the big question: if things do go south, can you still be emotionally stable? If the train goes off the rails, can you still be in control of yourself? Or will you get overwhelmed by anger, frustration, excitement, self-pity, or whatever else is your emotional danger zone?

You have to be able to say with 100% certainty that even if things go south, it won't be a problem. If you can't say that with certainty, it's just flirting with relapse for you to go.

7. *What's your 'out'—and will you be able to take it?*

In any risky situation in life, you've got to have an out—a back-up plan in case things don't work out.

If I'm buying a new house, I'll always ask myself: what happens if, God forbid, I lose my job and my finances tank? Would I be confident that I could rent the house if I need to? Or will I be able to sell it, and not lose money on it or have it sit on the market unsold for years?

In business, what's the plan in case things don't work out? Do I have a contingency plan for closing the business without going into personal bankruptcy?

Knowing your worst-case scenario plan ahead of time is vastly important, in any area of life. And it's no different in strategic planning to avoid relapse.

If you're at this wedding, and you realize that you're on the verge of your emotions getting the better of you, what's your plan to exit? Do you have your own car here? Could you call a cab, or is there someone you could count on to take you home?

And equally as important—will you be able to take that 'out'? Having a car won't help you if you know that you'd feel so guilty about leaving early that you wouldn't be able to bail when you need to.

Again, if you can't say with 100% certainty that you have a reliable back-up plan to exit from the situation, then it's just not worth the risk.

If you're not being honest here, you're just wasting your time

An important word of warning here. Remember back in Chapter Four when we talked about how all addicts are expert liars?

Well, it's entirely possible to bullshit your way through strategic planning. And if you let yourself do that, you can probably guess what the consequences will be.

Anyone who's ever been on a diet knows the truth of this. How easy is it for us to tell a story about how it really does make sense for us to eat that whole bag of Oreos? Maybe we're telling ourselves this is the *very last* bag of Oreos we'll ever eat. Or that we've been so strong in our diet, we can eat all these Oreos without them derailing us. Or hey, I read somewhere online that they have a new Oreo recipe and now they're actually really healthy!

All bullshit—and on some level, you know that.

So, as you're going through these steps of strategic planning, it's vital that you really walk through them honestly. Keep a wary eye out for when you start rationalizing lies. If you let yourself do that, the game is already lost. Be brutally honest.

"But Ross, this is my only chance to _____!"

There's another sneaky technique that your addict brain will use to get you tip-toeing your way toward relapse, and that's to tell yourself that the situation you're considering is something you just *have* to do.

I chose a family wedding in the example above for a reason. Hopefully, people only ever get married once, so yeah, it's a big deal. Weddings are really significant celebrations, and yes, it sucks to miss a wedding of a loved one.

But you have got to put your sobriety first.

If you go through the strategic planning steps and realize that Sally and Ted's wedding is too risky for your sobriety, that's got to be your priority.

And let's be real—is this your only opportunity to connect with Sally and Ted? It might be their only wedding, but these people are going to be your family for the rest of your life. Maybe you have to pass on their wedding, so instead you invite them out for a dinner when they get back from their honeymoon. You might feel like you're hurting their feelings by not attending their wedding, but if it meant you falling back into your addiction, do you really think they'd want you to come? Do you think they'd want you risking your sobriety just to spend a few hours at their wedding party?

Probably not.

Sure, there might be some people in your life that don't understand. Sometimes you'll have to avoid specific events to protect your sobriety, and other people just won't get it. Maybe you decide not to go to Sally and Ted's wedding, and Sally's mom gets pissed about it. But you know what? This is *your* ass on the line here, not theirs. It's your job to protect your sobriety, not theirs. You'll find that the vast majority of people will be completely understanding, but when some people aren't, don't let their shallow thinking risk your sobriety.

Make planning a habit

This all might sound at first like a lot of work just to decide whether or not you're going to a wedding, but this kind of strategic planning makes all the difference between being in the 95% of addicts that relapse or the 5% that can sustain sobriety.

The more you practice strategic planning, the better you'll get at it, and the easier it becomes. And remember, this habit is not just going to help you avoid falling back into addiction. When you're on a new diet, strategic planning will help you avoid finding yourself ravenously hungry at an all-you-can-eat pancake buffet party with no healthy options in sight. When you're trying to save money, strategic planning will help you avoid finding yourself out shopping with friends in a store where you can't resist costly impulse buys.

When you're planning strategically, you're setting yourself up to win—in every area of life.

Chapter Eighteen
(Don't) Show Me the Money

When addicts and counselors talk about triggers and enabling factors, there's one huge, green elephant in the room: money.

Whatever your addiction of choice, it almost certainly costs you money…probably a lot of money. It quite possibly costs you an insane amount of money that would make the average person gag in horror.

Money in your pocket is one of the most potent enabling forces addicts deal with. And most addicts, unless they get out of their addiction early, will end up blowing through savings, college accounts, mortgages, debt, and unpaid loans from friends and family. Addiction is voracious, and it'll take your finances down with you.

A silver spoon and a suicide vest

I tend to say that I didn't grow up with one silver spoon in my mouth—I grew up with two.

My father created a lot of success in the business world. When I was born, the youngest of my siblings by far, our family was blessed with a lot of wealth.

I was just a kid, 12 years old, when my dad died. Lymphoma took him after a five-year battle. At the time, I was just a mess of awkwardness and hormones, all the fun that puberty brings. Though my father amassed a fortune and left a mark on the world, I never really got the chance to know him.

My father's death threw my world upside down with change. One new surprise was access to money, made available through a trust. It was and is a huge blessing and opportunity that my father gave me, but it also came with its own dark side. Any addict who came from money will tell you that money doesn't solve all your problems—and it can make some of them a whole helluva lot worse.

When the second stage of my trust kicked in when I turned 30, I was swimming in money and drowning in addiction.

I bought so much cocaine that if I weren't smoking it all, I probably could have built a nice two-bedroom house with pure coke. I ended up moving to Lake Tahoe, and my life began imploding in spectacular, horrendous fashion. I rented an outrageous house to show off all that money, acting as though it was something I had earned myself, which it wasn't. I was like a pinch runner put on third who acts like he just hit a triple. I then proceeded to spend $1,800 a day on drugs. (For the friends and family of addicts who aren't familiar with the cost of drug habits, yes, that is an insane amount of drugs).

Getting the trust fund from my father was like a kid who doesn't know how to drive receiving a Ferrari for Christmas. It looks fun at first, but you know it's not going to end well.

I didn't realize what money really is. Money is a powerful force that can create a lot of good, but I chose to use it like a wrecking ball, demolishing my own life and the lives of those around me.

Money turned me into a real asshole, real fast. I didn't have the maturity to deal with it, and I didn't have the skills or know-how to handle it, so I turned it into a suicide vest. I loved it for all the wrong reasons, and abused the hell out of it. I thought it was making my whole life shine, but at the end of the day it just lit me on fire.

> # "The love of money is the root of all evil."
> ## 1 Timothy 6:10

Learning to tame the beast

Whatever your own addiction of choice, money is always the beast in the shadows. I deal with a lot of very wealthy families in my treatment programs, and they don't realize that there needs to be some serious money education in recovery. Old money or new money, it doesn't matter. Guidelines need to be established with guidance, care, and respect.

What exactly goes into your money management strategy depends largely on your unique situation, but there are some general rules that work pretty much across the board.

1. *Take inventory of your situation.*

What's your current financial situation?

How much money do you have right now—on hand, in accounts, et cetera? Do you currently have an income stream? If not, how can you plan to create income in ways that avoid old addiction-tied habits (so no, stealing and endlessly borrowing don't count here)?

What debts do you currently have, both 'official' debts and money you've borrowed from friends or family?

2. Distinguish between your 'needs' and your 'wants'.

When it comes to what you spend your money on, create a list of your 'needs' and 'wants'.

As a rule, you should find that your 'need' list is a whole lot more sparse than 'wants'. After all, what do you really need? Food, shelter, clothes on your back, resources to keep your recovery and sobriety going. That's pretty much the bare minimum. 'Wants' come in at different levels. For instance, reliable transportation is probably going to be a more pressing 'want' than, say, concert tickets. But it's useful to first break things into just two categories, and get clear on what you really *need* to move forward in life.

3. Create a budget.

How much are you going to spend each month? Week? Day? Where are you going to spend money in such a way that it matches your income? If at all possible, you should be budgeting some savings too, which leads us to…

4. Set short-term and long-term savings goals.

In the past, any extra money you could scrounge together was probably going to feed your addiction. Your goal is to be spending less each month than you're bringing in, but that extra money in your account can be dangerous if all you can think to spend it on is drugs and booze.

Now that you're planning a budget free of addiction, what are you going to be saving money for?

Here's where you can get more into your 'wants'. Maybe a short-term saving goal is to clear yourself of a hanging debt, or even something more fun like dancing classes. A long-term savings goal might be purchasing a car or putting a down payment on a house. Whatever your goals, the point is to create goals that motivate you, giving you that much more reason to *not* blow your money on your drug of choice.

And remember, these are about creating goals to work towards, not making impulsive buys then telling yourself, "Oh, that'll just count as my short-term goal today." Goals look toward the future, not instant gratification.

5. *Don't use debit or credit cards; use strictly budgeted cash.*

It might seem like an inconvenience, but staying cash-only with a strict budget is hugely important. One tried-and-true strategy is to turn your budget into a cash envelope system. At the start of every month or every week, fill envelopes with cash for budgeted items. When the envelope runs out, that's it.

As much as possible, automate your finances. If you have a job that can set up direct deposit, do it. That way you won't be tempted to cash a check in your hands. If you can set up your recurring bills to deduct automatically from your bank account, do it.

Limit how much cash you carry on your person to what you'll actually need for the day. Not having a debit card will prevent you from impulsive (and dangerous) ATM withdrawals. If you need more money for a legitimate reason, go to a bank and wait in line. That extra step of inconvenience will prevent a lot of impulsive choices you'll regret later.

6. *Don't do it alone.*

As with most everything in recovery, don't do this alone. If you've never been responsible with money and all of this is freaking you out, that's ok. There are resources out there for you to lean on.

If you have friends or family you trust who are good at money management, ask them to help you out here. There are also a ton of free money-management tools and apps out there. Use them.

With great power...

Money is always going to play a central role in your life, unless you decide to become a penniless monk. Crash-and-burn spending used to feed your addiction, but it doesn't have to now. Learning and practicing the skills of money management are going to build the sober life you want, brick by brick. Take a deep breath, and take it one brick at a time.

Chapter Nineteen
The Power of a Job

I first experienced rehab treatment programs as a patient. Today, my career is built around helping thousands of other addicts dig themselves out of the trenches of addiction. But I didn't make that jump in one single leap.

Since completing my final, lasting stint in an inpatient program, I've worked every single job that exists in treatment today. Now, let me be clear—I don't mean that I've worked a lot of them, or that I worked the 'glamorous' jobs at a lot of places. I mean that I've worked in *all* the jobs.

My first job in a treatment center was as a landscaper at a Malibu rehab facility. I cut the lawn. I dug holes for trees. I planted trees and cut trees down. I hung dry wall and changed light bulbs. I drove a backhoe, broke ground with a pickaxe, and at one point literally dug a hole for an entire septic system. It was a really big hole.

Later on, I found myself working as an admissions coordinator. In that position, I exchanged some choice words with my boss because I thought that what he was telling people on the phone was crap. I got fired from that one, but kept working in different positions. It wasn't always at the same treatment center (though I did end up working back at the place I'd gotten fired from), but I kept at it, job after job, position after position.

Eventually I was given a counselor position. It was amazing—I had my own office, my own clients. I started running group sessions. They sucked at first, and anyone that attended one can tell you that. But I kept at it, day after day, building my skills and expertise, until reaching the point where I'm at today.

Those years working all those jobs served me in many ways.

First, I got to see the treatment industry inside and out. I saw it from every angle imaginable. I saw both what was working and what was not working. That experience is what made it possible for me to found Rebos and help so many people since.

But that work served me in a whole other field of ways—because getting a job, pretty much any job, is vital for recovering addicts.

> # Don't underestimate the power of a job to change your life.

A job is one of your golden tickets

There are some things you can do in your early recovery that will benefit you across the board. Working a job is one of the biggest.

You might come out of inpatient care with a job already, one that you took a leave from to go into treatment. Or maybe, for whatever reason, your treatment has been outpatient from the get-go, and you've been working a job the whole while. Or maybe, like many recovering addicts, you haven't worked in a while. Addiction can make it almost impossible to hold down a job.

Whatever your situation, it's vital that you begin working a job as soon as possible in your outpatient time—and if you already have a job, you get to dive in with new vigor. The benefits go on and on, but here are a choice few:

1. Learning the value of a dollar, and building your accounts

Like we discussed in the previous chapter, a dysfunctional relationship with money is at the heart of addictions of all sorts.

Odds are, your personal finances at this point are a mess. You've probably been spending any money you get your hands on to fill your addiction of choice. You might be in debt with credit cards and banks or have a daunting list of unpaid loans from friends and family.

If you're like me, there's a good chance that you don't really understand the value of a dollar at this point in your life.

A job is your ticket to change all of that.

Let me tell you—when I was digging holes in the hot Southern California sun for my money, you'd better believe I learned a whole new appreciation for each dollar. Suddenly, money meant something to me it hadn't before. It represented value, hard work, effort, and sweat. The more you value the money in your pocket, the better choices you'll make with that money.

Plus, there's the simple reality that financial stability requires income. You're not going to start paying off your debts and reaching financial security until you start bringing some money in.

2. The structure of a work schedule

When you're starting a new post-addiction life, structure is key. The more you've structured and planned out every hour of every day, the less likely it is that you'll fall into relapse. You're going through massive changes in your life and within yourself, and a concrete daily structure to follow is the foundation you need to make all those changes.

With a job, a huge chunk of your time becomes structured. You know exactly where you have to be from 9am to 5pm, Monday through Friday (or whatever the days and hours are for your particular job).

3. Finding purpose and fulfillment

Human beings have a natural psyche that is hard-wired to seek out purpose and fulfillment. We need to be needed, to have a sense of accomplishment. A job will provide this for you.

Now, especially when you're taking these first steps into sober living, your job might not be your highest calling or the vocation of your dreams. But that doesn't mean you won't find purpose and fulfillment in it. Digging holes and mowing lawns wasn't my life's dream job, but that didn't matter. I had a purpose, I had tasks to complete, and with each hole that I dug or lawn that I mowed, I enjoyed that boost of accomplishment.

When we're stuck in addiction, our focus is all self-centered—everything revolves around our need to feed the addiction, like a black hole pulling in everything around it.

With a job, you start to focus your energy outside of yourself. Even if you're flipping burgers at a fast food joint, you're focusing outwards, being in service to others. No matter your job, you'll find that this sense of purpose and accomplishment begins to fill parts of yourself that drugs or alcohol never could.

4. Connecting with community

For a lot of recovering addicts, sobriety means a loss of community. You're not going to be going to parties every night, hanging out at the casino after work every day, or lighting up with your favorite drug dealer. But, human beings are social creatures, and you've got to have a community around you.

A job will start to build this new community in your life. There's nothing quite like the camaraderie of coworkers, whether in a Fortune 500 company or washing dishes in a restaurant.

This is one area that brings to light the fact that not all jobs are equal for the recovering addict. It doesn't matter whether your job is a desk job that pays great or a burger-flipping job that pays minimum wage. But it does matter that your workplace community isn't entirely focused on the sources of your addiction. You'll probably have coworkers who drink wine with dinner or have a few beers over the weekend, but you don't want to work in a bar.

It probably goes without saying, but don't choose a job that's centered on your old addiction habits. If you were a gambling addict, don't take a job as a blackjack dealer. You get the picture.

Put your sobriety first—and listen to your counselors

Now that we've laid out all the benefits of getting a job, it's time to put one big asterisk on the end. All of these benefits of a job are absolutely true—*when* it's the right time for you to do so.

For a lot of people, the first weeks and even months of treatment are going to be a time when therapy and counseling and the basics of sober life are going to be a full-time job. As you move forward, it's vital that you be in communication with your counselors and therapists about when the time is right for you to start working a job. Sometimes counselors will tell you, "Ok, I think you're ready to start working, but for now start out with just a part-time job, and we'll move you up to full-time work a little later on." Other times, they'll encourage you to get full-time employment right when you leave inpatient treatment.

Remember, there is no one-size-fits-all timing with any of this stuff. Successful treatment programs are all about customization and finding the solutions that are a perfect match for your particular circumstances.

As with everything else, be in communication with your counselors and therapists—and follow their guidance.

The first rungs of a new ladder

Again, when you're taking these first steps in your new sober life, it's not the time to worry about launching into the career of your dreams or finding a job that pays a million a year.

You have years ahead of you to develop a career. Now is the time to build a solid, sturdy foundation.

Chapter Twenty
Living Beyond the Quick Fix

Let me paint a picture for you. It's my first round in a rehab center. I'm in one of the biggest, oldest, best-reputed treatment centers in the country. A couple days ago, I was sitting in an intervention with my family, surrounded by seven family members telling me basically, "You know what, Ross? We love you, but you're being a piece of shit, and you've been a piece of shit for a long time."

After that oh-so-fun intervention, I was packed onto a plane with a one-way ticket to check into a rehab center with no discharge date in sight. I spent that first night sleeping on rubber sheets in a room with a guy that snored like nobody's business. Seriously, it was like trying to sleep next to a freight train. On rubber sheets. In a rehab center for the first time.

Needless to say, I didn't get any sleep that night.

So here I am, feeling like utter crap with my new psychiatrist sitting across from me. The doctor's got a sheet of paper on a clipboard, and he starts asking me a bunch of questions. What's my sleeping pattern like? How do I feel right now? Do I feel depressed?

I tell the doc the truth. I didn't sleep well the night before. I feel really sad and crappy right now. I don't exactly have a rosy outlook on my life right now. And yeah, I'm feeling pretty depressed.

While I'm talking, the psychiatrist is checking off boxes on his paper, nodding along. Just minutes later, after we've gone through these superficial questions and answers, he tells me I've got a sleeping disorder and am depressed, and so he writes me two prescriptions—one for sleeping medication and one for an antidepressant.

Wait—what?

We didn't talk about *why* I'm feeling the way I am right now, or *why* I slept like crap last night. We didn't talk about any other ways that I could start processing or working through what I'm dealing with.

He just had a list with questions on one side, and diagnoses on the other side. Bada-bing bada-boom, check…check…check, have a couple new prescriptions.

A big ol' caveat

Before we go any further in this chapter, we've got to add a big Barry Bonds asterisk here. There are absolutely, without a doubt, many medical conditions that require pharmaceutical intervention. Many of these are psychiatric conditions—including some of the conditions that I'll talk about here.

I've said it before already, but let me say it again—I am not a doctor. Everyone catch that? I am not a doctor. I'm not trying to tell you to take my advice over a doctor's, to ignore your doctor's advice, or to (God forbid) stop seeing doctors.

Everyone clear?

Ok, let's move forward.

> # "It always seems impossible until it's done."
>
> ## - Nelson Mandela

A cultural addiction to drugs and instant fixes

Our culture, as a whole, is addicted to instant fixes. How many times have you seen a get-rich-quick scheme in an internet ad? Or a 'lose 20 pounds in one week *secret diet plan*' (just eat bananas! or don't eat bananas!)? Or an eliminate-your-wrinkles-overnight secret that dermatologists supposedly hate?

One instant fix after another.

And let's be honest, even when you *know* that those instant-fix internet schemes are total bull, a little part of you is saying, "But man, I wish that would work..."

That instant-gratification fix is in full force when it comes to pills.

Want to lose that weight? We've got a pill for you—no exercise required.

Things not perfect in the bedroom? We've got pills for that.

Low energy at work? We've got a whole aisle of pills for that.

You know it's only a matter of time before someone starts hocking get-rich-quick pills.

It's the same with how we relate to medicine—and how the medical industry relates to us. If you go into the doctor's office for an annual checkup and the doctor tells you that your borderline high blood pressure is now really high blood pressure, their first response is probably going to be to start writing you a prescription for blood pressure medicine. But you know what would happen if you said, "Hey doc, I know I need to get this under control, but I'd rather avoid medication if possible and handle it through lifestyle changes. What could I start doing on my own to lower my blood pressure?"

Your doctor would probably blink a few times in shock, then start telling you about exercises and diet changes to get your blood pressure back down to safe levels. Because here's the thing—doctors are quick to give us the easy-fix medication solution because *that's what we've been conditioned to want.* Doctors know that if they tell all of their patients the lifestyle changes they need to make for their health, the vast majority of those patients just won't put the effort in. They'll either ask for pharmaceutical fixes right away, or nod their heads in the doctor's office then go home and change nothing.

Sobriety and instant gratification don't mix

The effects of this come full-force for addicts taking their first steps into a sober life.

Addicts have spent months, years, decades, sometimes their entire life since high school, taking the instant-gratification fix. Especially with drugs and alcohol, the addiction usually takes over pretty much every aspect of their lives. How do alcoholics learn to go to sleep? Drink until you literally pass out. How do drug addicts process and cope with difficult situations in life? Pop more pills or do a few extra lines.

When you're learning to live sober, you're not just learning how to not drink a bottle of wine every night, or not wake up to a gram of cocaine. You also have to literally learn how to fall asleep sober. How to feel your feelings and process your emotions sober. How to enjoy life sober. How to deal with hardship sober. How to eat three meals a day sober. How to talk to your family sober. How to hold a job sober. How to do just about anything—sober.

If you take an addict fresh out of detox and give them a diagnostic questionnaire, I can guarantee you that every one of them could be diagnosed with some sort of medical condition. Probably all of them could fit the bill for sleeping disorders. Most for depression, or anxiety, or ADD, or all of the above.

And look—I'm sure some of these addicts *do* have serious medical conditions that require pharmaceutical intervention. Sometimes clinical depression really is just a matter of brain chemistry being out of whack, and antidepressants are necessary. Sometimes ADD is impossible to live with, without medication.

But do we really think that *all* of these addicts, fresh off detox, need all these drugs? Or is it possible, just maybe, that some of these people would be better off learning how to live without drugs?

Learning to live sober

The last time I was in treatment, I had one counselor who really opened my eyes to a lot of this.

I can remember one moment in particular. I was standing by the door when he came up and asked me what I was waiting for. I told him I was waiting for a ride to the doctor's office to get a refill on my ADD medication.

"Why are you taking that?" he asked me.

"Well, I was diagnosed with ADD," I said.

"So?" he asked again. "Look, you might well have ADD that needs to be medicated. But have you ever not done drugs of some sort? Have you ever gotten off everything, and really felt what it's like to be you? Have you ever learned to drive yourself? What if you first tried to work with and live with the ADD you've been diagnosed with?"

This blew my mind.

It was literally the month the iPhone came out. Later, this same guy was talking to me again, and pulled out his brand-new iPhone. "This phone was designed by a guy with ADD, Steve Jobs," he said. "Can you imagine if this guy were medicated? I wouldn't have this amazing gadget in my pocket. What if learning to live with your ADD would make something like this possible?"

I won't beat around the bush here. When I was in treatment for the last time, learning to live free of *all* drugs, it wasn't always easy. For the first month and a half, every night, I'd be lying wide awake at 3am. But I wouldn't freak out—I'd embrace it. I knew that I was in training to not be a drug addict, literally training my body and my mind to fall asleep naturally.

And bottom line, it's not fast. When you've spent years pumping all of these substances into your body, it takes time to train yourself to do them organically, time to recalibrate your body. Sure, maybe you'll discover that you are dealing with a condition that does require pharmaceuticals. But until you find your baseline and work on living organically and drug-free, you can't know that for sure.

This nitty-gritty work, like learning how to actually fall asleep, might not be glamorous, but it's all part of sobriety.

It might not be the instant-gratification quick fix we're all trained to want, but it's the fix that will last.

Chapter Twenty-One
What's Your Tell?

I went to treatment for drugs and alcohol, but first I went to treatment for being an arrogant ass.

Everyone tends to develop alternate egos, different versions of themselves that they play in different situations. At one point, like I've mentioned earlier, I figure that I had an even dozen different versions of Ross that I'd pull out for different situations.

One of those alternate egos, though, caused me more trouble than the rest of them combined. That alternate ego became my first-class, one-way ticket straight to addiction. That alternate ego played such a huge, formative role in my life—for better and worse—that it had its own name:

Thurston Howell III.

The name might sound familiar, or you might even recognize it off the bat. Thurston was "The Millionaire" from *Gilligan's Island*—the most arrogant, pompous guy I could think of. Thurston Howell III was filthy rich, and his wealth was only surpassed by how arrogantly he flaunted it. Thurston even once made the *Forbes Fictional 15* list of the 15 richest fictional characters—right behind Willy Wonka.

This alternate ego of mine was a master of the fine art of arrogance, just like Thurston from *Gilligan's Island*. But whereas the fictional character had at least made his own money as the founder and president of countless businesses, my alternate ego was arrogant for access to wealth that I hadn't even created. Like

I've talked about earlier, this was my "pinch runner put on third base acting like he hit a triple" alter ego.

Thurston was the version of myself that had to be the biggest, baddest, craziest guy at parties. The guy who had to be the drunkest and highest, who had to throw the wildest parties at the hippest houses just to show off how rich and awesome he thought he was. Thurston was the alter ego that took those first steps on the road to addiction.

Like I said, my addiction became about drugs and alcohol, but at its core it was rooted in arrogance.

What was a danger then is a danger now

My "Thurston" ego, and the arrogance that it represents, was a danger to me then and is still a danger to me now.

I know that if I ever relapse, it will be Thurston's arrogance that paves the way. So, in my daily life, I know that I have to keep a watchful eye open and avoid arrogance where it might crop it.

I'll be honest. These days, I could have any car that I want. Sports cars, flashy cars, the sorts of cars that scream success. But you know what I drive? A Toyota 4Runner. Because I know that, even with all the years of work I've put in, driving a flashy car would go to my head. It would feed that arrogance, which would lead nowhere good.

Learn to read yourself, and you won't catch yourself by surprise.

Arrogance is my 'tell'—so, what's yours?

Arrogance is the trait or behavior that's at the core of my addiction. Because of this, I know that if arrogance starts creeping more and more into my life—if Thurston starts showing up more often—that I'm starting to play with fire. When I'm starting to act more arrogantly, my danger for relapse rises with it.

In that way, arrogance is my 'tell'—the clue that can warn me that I'm starting down a dangerous path towards relapse.

It's just like in poker, where a player's tell is the unconscious behavior that broadcasts whether they've got a winning hand or a crappy bluff. If you learn to read a poker player's tell, you can know how the hands will turn out. If you learn to read an addict's tell, you can know when relapse danger is ticking up.

Arrogance is my 'tell'—but that's only my particular case.

Odds are there's a different trait or behavior that led the way for you into addiction, and which now represents your 'tell' that a relapse danger might be approaching. Maybe for you, that 'tell' is isolating yourself, pushing others away. There are a whole bunch of possible traits it might be. Some common tells to consider are:

- Selfishness
- Jealousy
- Resentment
- Anger
- Arrogance
- Isolation
- Judgment
- Self-pity
- Depression
- Anxiety
- Recklessness

All of us encounter these traits and behaviors at times, but you've got to look inside—and look at your past—to discover which trait or behavior was most at the root of your path into addiction. Whatever that is, that's your tell.

And remember—whatever your 'problem trait' is when it comes to addiction, it is also what's probably holding you back throughout other areas of your life. If jealousy is the behavior trait that gets you on the path to addiction, you can bet that it's screwing up other areas of your life too.

For me, arrogance wasn't just a problem with addiction. It also got in the way of me having fulfilling personal relationships with my family, friends, and romantic partners. When you identify your 'tell' and start keeping a keen eye out for it, you'll start to discover how it was disrupting other areas of your life—and how you can fix that.

Because again, sobriety is all about spiritual profitability. And spiritual profitability is about living a fulfilling, enriched, successful life in every area.

Being on alert, and being in communication

Now that you know your tell, you've got to keep a vigilant watch for it. Self-awareness is a huge part of sober living, and it comes into play big-time here. As you periodically reflect on your days and weeks, doing your self-checkins, ask yourself, "Is my 'tell' showing up again?"

In my case, this means being on the lookout for arrogance. Has my arrogant side been showing up again? Is Thurston coming out to play more than I'm comfortable with?

Like so much of lifelong relapse prevention, this is all about continual, evolving work. You get to develop this self-awareness as a habit.

But you know what? You can't do this alone.

Like with so much of sobriety, being on guard for your 'tell' is something that you need to do with a team around you.

When I'm working as a counselor with families, I always tell them that family sessions are not just about mending fences. Yes, we're here to heal wounds and rebuild bridges, but that's not all of it. We're also here to create strategies to prevent relapse and support sobriety. Addiction is in many ways a family issue—and so is sustainable sobriety.

All of us have blind spots about ourselves and our behaviors—aspects of ourselves that we're unable to see on our own. You can never see the back of your head without mirrors, and in a similar way, you can never be fully aware of how you're acting, simply because you're the one doing the acting.

This is where your support team comes in, and family will usually be at the front lines here.

When I work with a couple in counseling, I always make sure both parties understand this. If a husband and wife are in front of me and the husband is the one struggling with addiction, I'll say to him, "Look, I'm going to call you out right now for your wife. These are the telltale signs that she needs to watch out for, and you need to be ok with that. When she sees them, she needs to speak up and you need to listen. It might just be a nudge on the elbow or a quiet word in your ear, but there needs to be that open communication."

Imagine I'm sitting with you at a restaurant, eating a sandwich. While we're eating and talking, you notice that I've got a blob of sauce on the side of my mouth. You're probably going to say, "Hey Ross, you've got a little something there." I'm not going to cuss you out or deny it or storm away from the table in a huff. I'm going to pick up my napkin, wipe my mouth, say "Thanks!" and then move on. It's the exact same concept here.

You need to learn that your family is looking out for you—but your family also needs to learn how to communicate with you.

Oftentimes, family and friends of addicts have built up so much resentment and anger at the addict's behavior that at the first sign of them slipping back, those family and friends will just lash out. That reaction is understandable, but not productive.

Imagine we're sitting at a table again, and I've got sauce on my face. What would happen if you were to just grit your teeth and bark at me, "Goddamn it Ross, you're such a slob. It's humiliating to be with you when you're such a mess like this, can you just get your act together?"

Obviously, this is going to hit me on a much more personal level. I'm probably going to lash back at you, and we'll argue back and forth until one of us storms away. And on top of that, I still don't know that I have sauce on my face! In this example, you've communicated your opinions and feelings, but not what you're actually noticing—so you're not giving me any room to fix the situation on my end.

The same dynamics are at play when it comes to identifying and communicating relapse warning signs. Addicts need to learn to be open to feedback when people close to them start noticing their 'tells' and alarm bells start ringing. At the same time, the people close to addicts need to learn how to communicate what they're seeing with compassion and productivity.

It's a dance, and it might take a little practice, but learning the steps will make it all that much harder for relapse to sneak up on you. Arm yourself with awareness and communication, and you'll be equipped to defend your sobriety.

Chapter Twenty-Two
Stop Counting Down, Start Building Up

One of the most insane practices found throughout the world of treatment today is the idea of counting days down.

You'll first encounter it when you step foot inside an inpatient center. Half the patients there will just literally be counting down the days until they leave. Two weeks to go! One week to go! Just three more days to go! Another few hours and I'm out of here!

This is the most ridiculous idea for addicts to take on—and these treatment centers are just feeding the beast.

I've seen counselors at treatment centers throw a huge party for patients at the end of a 28-day program. This is crazy to me. Yes, 28 days clean is a miracle and a true accomplishment. You've broken a pattern and have started to heal. But these people aren't treating that 28-day mark as a starting-off point; they're treating it like some sort of final accomplishment.

And we wonder why so many addicts relapse and collapse back into addiction?

Let me put it this way. When we're "counting down the days," we're literally creating a "countdown." The word is right there in the first phrase.

When I say "countdown," what do you imagine? Maybe one of those digital clocks attached to a bomb, as seen in every action movie ever made. Counting down until the detonation, the explosion, the worst-case-scenario doomsday moment. And this is how we want to think about and talk about sobriety? Seriously?

Or maybe when you hear "countdown," you imagine something like the New Year's countdown, when everyone at the party counts down those final ten seconds of December 31st, before cheering on the start of the next year.

This kind of symbolism is better than a bomb, but it's still terrible for the work of sobriety. When you imagine sobriety like this kind of countdown, you get the idea that if you just reach some arbitrary point, the work will be done. You get addicts thinking "If I just make it to *then*, I'll be in the clear and get this crap behind me." But that's not how life works, folks.

What happens at the end of 28 days? You start day 29. You either continue developing your sobriety and spiritual profitability, or you start to slide backwards. It's one or the other. There's no point where the work of sobriety is complete, and so there's never any time where it makes sense to count down the days. This kind of thinking just sets addicts up for failure and relapse.

> # "Do the best you can until you know better. Then when you know better, do it better."
> ## - Maya Angelou

Start building up instead

You might be saying to yourself, "Ross, why are you being such a party pooper? Can't I celebrate these sorts of accomplishments? Don't AA meetings give out chips when you're 30 days sober, or 90 days sober, and so on?"

Absolutely.

Don't get me wrong, it is wonderful and useful to celebrate milestones on your road of sobriety. And yes, reaching these milestones is a huge accomplishment. But it's all about how you're visualizing those accomplishments, and how you think about them. Don't count down the days. Instead, think about yourself as building an ever-growing sober empire.

Remember, you want to be running your sobriety like you'd run a business. Do you think successful businesses count down the days until they hit their first month or first year in business, then throw a big party and close up shop because they're 'finished'? No, of course not.

But do businesses celebrate reaching their first profitable month? Or their first six months of business, or their first year, or first decade? Absolutely.

These accomplishments are milestones on a journey. But they're milestones on a journey that always has a next step, a tomorrow, a "further to go from here." And that's a good thing!

Would you want to run a business that had an upper limit on how profitable it could be, or a countdown to when it would expire? Probably not. You'd want to run a business that was growing each day, becoming increasingly profitable every quarter.

And the same is true for your sober life. Sobriety is a continuous journey of growth and increasing spiritual profitability, with no upper limit to how far you can take it.

Now *that's* something worth celebrating.

Creating wins every day

Let me make it clear—I'm all about honoring accomplishments and milestones, all about creating wins for yourself that you can celebrate.

In fact, I don't just want you creating and celebrating victories every 30 days or every 90 days. I want you creating these wins *every single day.*

This is one of the most awesome parts of sobriety and one of those golden keys to making the journey sustainable—and fun.

Yes, sobriety can be fun. People don't say that enough.

When you're in this journey of lifelong relapse prevention and personal development, you get to be creating a win in your life every day, creating new spiritual profit every day.

One day that might be a win with your therapist, when you uncover a new, deep truth about yourself. Another day that win might be in your relationships, when you create intimacy and connection on a level you've never experienced yet. Another day that win might be completing a big project at work, one that you never could have even started when you were buried in addiction. Another day, that win might be as simple as playing a game of pick-up basketball with friends and having an absolute blast.

The list goes on and on.

When you're creating and acknowledging wins every day, you stay energized and invested and committed. This is true everywhere in life. In your career, keep creating wins. Projects successfully accomplished, raises in your paycheck, awards won, client interactions that went really well. From big to small, build those victories every day. Same goes for your health, your relationships, your finances, everything.

Remember, emotional sobriety is all about experiencing life organically, and spiritual profitability is all about finding your rhythm in life, loving and accepting yourself, and grooving into your place in the world. When you're investing in these things, day in and day out, life gets more and more awesome.

So, create those wins, and celebrate the heck out of them. Creating and celebrating victories just builds up your dedication to continue the work—and makes the work that much more enjoyable. It's this amazing positive feedback loop. The more you win, the more you win.

And doesn't that sound like a lifelong journey worth taking?

Chapter Twenty-Three
Your Story: Own the Past, Write the Future

When I look back on my life, I can honestly say that becoming a drug addict was one of the greatest things to happen to me. I can see your eyebrows shooting up from here, but I'm serious.

If I hadn't become a hardcore addict, I wouldn't have had the literally life-or-death motivation to turn my life around for the better. I wouldn't have created the Rebos Treatment Centers, and so wouldn't have been able to help thousands of people overcome their own addiction struggles. I wouldn't have the joyful, spiritually profitable life that I enjoy now. Heck, I probably wouldn't have met or married my wife.

Now obviously, I'm not trying to say drug addiction is a good thing. It's not something I recommend to people. In fact, if anyone asked me, I'd pretty emphatically recommend they *not* become a raving drug addict. (Hopefully this doesn't surprise you at this point in the book.)

What I am saying is that your past experiences are neutral until you give them meaning. You get to choose what your future looks like, and part of that means choosing how to define the past.

If you want to be the one writing your life's story, you've got to accept and embrace every part of the story that's already been written. Accept and embrace the parts of your life that were happy, and accept and embrace the parts that were difficult and painful. If I never embraced my history as a drug addict, I wouldn't be able to create the best future possible.

The Rebos buffalo

When you go to pretty much any addiction programs or meetings, you'll get some sort of physical token for your time there, maybe a coin, maybe a chip. At Rebos, we developed our own tokens: pewter chips with our buffalo logo on them.

The buffalo is our logo—our spirit animal of sorts—because I've found that the path and destiny of a buffalo has a lot of similarities with the journey of addicts trying to change their lives.

One of the times that I found myself in treatment, I had only one book to read, a book on animal totems. That's when the buffalo really hit me as a symbol of this journey we're on.

Buffalos know their environment, they know what they're capable of, and they go through life fully in tune with both.

In the warm months, buffalos are on the move, hustling around, grazing, mating, all that good stuff. But they always travel as a herd. Why? Because they know there are predators out there, and they know they're safer in numbers. Survival instincts.

You might see buffalos hustling around in the warm months, but you'll almost never see them booking it in the winter. Why? Because the snow is too deep, which makes it way more strenuous to run, and when buffalo do run in the snow, they will literally have a heart attack from the exertion and die. They know that about themselves, so they don't do it.

Buffalo symbolize the journey of recovery and transformation even more in their relationship with Native Americans and how Native American tribes think about them and interact with them. When native tribes hunt and kill buffalo, they use every piece of the animal. No one part of the buffalo is more valuable than another—it's one whole package that the natives use entirely. The 'ugly' pieces are just as valuable and honored as the 'pretty' parts. The beat-up hooves are just as valuable as the hide.

To succeed in this journey of recovery and personal transformation, you've got to treat your life's story the same way.

> # Control your destiny, or someone else will.

Owning and honoring your entire story

If you want to really be in control of your life, to choose the direction and shape of your future, then you've got to own your life story—all of it.

In my life story, my worst nightmare from childhood has just as much value as my wedding day. Sure, I'm probably not going to hang pictures of my nightmares on the wall, but I have to keep it and own it, hold it close and remember it, learn from it, grow from it.

Some moments in your life are painful, like shards of glass from a shattered mirror. They hurt when held, are unpleasant to recollect, and can cause pain to yourself or others.

But they're still part of your story.

You're only truly the author of your life when you take ownership of the entire story. When you hold yourself accountable for every choice you've made, every action you've taken, and the 'why' behind all of them.

If you aren't the author of your life, you're just a judgmental reader. And guess what? Judgmental readers don't get to write the next book in the series.

Your past is defined by the meaning you give it

I'm going to tell you about a close neighbor and friend of mine, Dario Gabbai.

At the time I'm writing this, Dario is 95 years old. He was born in Greece in 1922, to a Jewish family.

When Dario was just 21 years old, he and his entire family were taken by the Nazis and sent to Auschwitz. When they got there, the family was separated into two lines. Dario, his brother, and two of his cousins were sent to one line, and the rest of his whole family was sent to another line, selected for execution. Dario had to watch while his parents and most of his family were put onto trucks headed for the gas chambers.

But the nightmare was just beginning.

Everyone in concentration camps was forced into some sort of labor. Dario, along with his brother and cousins, was selected for something called the Sonderkommando. This small group of prisoners was forced to work in the gas chambers themselves. When a new group of victims was sent in, Dario had to help them undress, all the while keeping up the illusion that they were just going in for showers.

When the gas turned on, Dario could hear the screams.

When the killing was done, Dario and the rest of the Sonderkommando were forced to go in, remove the bodies, and wash the chambers. Then the nightmare would begin again. Dario had to do this for nearly nine months until he was rescued, and he estimates that he was forced to witness the slaughter of 600,000 Jews.

Dario had to live a terror that none of us could even imagine.

After the war, Dario moved to the United States, eventually settling down in California. Every night—and whenever he closed his eyes—Dario was haunted by nightmares of what he'd been through. For years, he tried to push the memories away, tried to forget what was impossible to forget, tried to distance himself from what he'd been through. And who could blame him? But the nightmares kept coming.

Things finally changed when Dario changed his strategy. Instead of trying to forget and push away the horror that he'd been through, he accepted and embraced what his life had been. And because he accepted the entirety of his life's story, he turned it into something great.

Dario became one of the world's most outspoken survivors of the Holocaust, sharing his story around the world. His willingness to accept and share his story has brought immense value to millions. He brings healing, as well as lessons the world needs to hear. He's been featured in a number of documentaries, including Steven Spielberg's Holocaust documentary, "The Last Days."

Dario had the courage to choose to be the author of his life's story, even after the unimaginable horrors of the Holocaust. And because he did, he's provided immense value to the world—and he's able to enjoy life again.

You've got some ugly moments in your past. Not the horror that Dario went through, but horrors and hardships of your own.

And you know what? You get to decide what all of those moments mean. They could mean you're a broken failure and there's no point even trying, or they could be the inspiration that led to your greatness.

When you own your story, it's totally up to you.

143

Chapter Twenty-Four
Just Because You're Changing Doesn't Mean Others Are

There's something I hear a lot from recovering addicts who are a few months into their sobriety and back in the outside world interacting with friends and family.

A patient will walk into my office, clearly frustrated and fuming inside. Something's obviously on their mind, and they aren't happy about it. So, I ask them what's going on, and they launch right in.

"It's my damn family!" they'll say. "Here I am doing all of this work on myself, doing everything they've been saying for years that I should do, and it's like none of it matters to them. They're still treating me like the crazy out-of-control addict. They're not giving me the benefit of the doubt or accommodating me at all. Why can't they be more supportive?!"

At this point, I'll take a deep breath. I know the person in front of me wants me to agree with them, wants me to say that I'll call their family in right away to set them straight, because yeah, it's so unfair that they're still being treated like that.

But you know what? I can't say that, because that's not how life works.

Just because you're changing doesn't mean others are—and even though that might be frustrating, it's important that you accept that.

They're still seeing the old you, and seeing the new you takes time

How long were you stuck in the trenches of addiction? Months? Years? Decades even?

In all of that time, you were training the people around you to treat you as an addict. However you acted as an addict, that's how your family learned to see you. It sucks, but it's just how it is.

Remember, addiction is a family disease. Because even if they weren't the ones going crazy with drugs or alcohol, your addiction has impacted their emotions and actions. Their lives have been affected too.

When you make a huge change like sobriety and come back as a whole new version of yourself, it takes time for the people around you to adjust. Yes, they will learn to see the 'new you,' but it doesn't happen overnight. It requires you showing up as the new you consistently, in big ways and little ways, over time. After a few dozen conversations where you aren't blowing up at them in anger, they'll start to see that as your new normal. After a few months have gone by without you stealing money from them, maybe they'll be able to start trusting you again.

Repairing relationships takes time. Regaining trust takes time. Showing people that they can count on you again takes time.

It might feel frustrating, but this is an opportunity for you to put your ego aside and be considerate and compassionate for where your family is. It's an opportunity to accept the uncomfortable truth of how your addiction has affected the people around you, and understand that healing all of that is a journey.

This was all definitely true for me and my own journey of sobriety.

When I completed inpatient treatment for the last time, my family had already seen me relapse dozens and dozens of times.

They'd watched me start to get my life together, only to have things fall apart again, worse and worse. So yeah, they were skeptical. Very skeptical.

At first, I'd get frustrated about it. Didn't they see me jumping through all of these hoops? Didn't they understand that I was trying to turn my life around? Why couldn't we all just hit a big 'reset' button?

But finally, I turned the volume down on my ego and started practicing a little humility and understanding. I'd put these people through hell. I'd given them every reason to be skeptical. So, if it takes them time to come around and start trusting me again, that's totally ok.

In the end, some family members came around quickly, and others not so quickly. Some were more understanding, some less so. Frankly there might be some who still are skeptical even after more than a decade.

And that's ok. If it takes 20 minutes, it takes 20 minutes. If it takes 20 years, it takes 20 years. I'm in this for the long haul.

Be your own hero.

You've been doing deep inner work—but not everyone around you has

Addiction recovery is intense.

When done right, in the ways that I've laid out in these pages, 30 days of treatment is like going through a year of personal therapy. You're learning things about yourself that you never realized before. You're gaining new perspectives on your past, on how you operate, on how events and circumstances have affected you.

You're learning new ways of thinking and new ways of relating to yourself and the world around you.

But guess what: in those same 30 days, your family and friends have probably just been going about their normal, day-to-day lives.

Sure, maybe they've joined you for a couple one-hour sessions with your counselor or therapist. Then again, maybe they haven't. But even if they did, that's nothing compared to the inner work and transformation that you've gone through.

You're in a whole new space—but they aren't. And like it or not, it's not fair or reasonable for you to expect otherwise.

Imagine you just went on a week-long health retreat, where you learned things about your body and mind that you never knew before. You've adopted an entirely new diet, started a new exercise regime, and have committed to your health and physical wellness in a whole new way.

Then you go home. Your husband or wife wants to go out to the same restaurants that only serve those deliciously fatty and salty meals you both used to love. Your friends still want to just hang out on the couch, watching sports and eating nachos. You want to eat healthy and be active, but everyone else in your life is still in the same place they were before you (and only you) went on that week-long health retreat.

Would it be fair or reasonable for you to get pissed at your spouse for wanting to go to the same restaurants you two used to go to? Would it be fair for you to get pissed at your friends for wanting to hang out in the ways you've always hung out?

Of course not.

Sure, you might hope to eventually shift how your spouse thinks about food too. You might want him or her to join you in your new diet plan. And yeah, maybe you'll want to get your friends off the couch and start playing sports with you instead of just watching it on TV. That's all great. But it also takes time.

The same is true when you're making all of this inner progress in your addiction treatment. You're seeing and living life in a whole new way now, and you're probably discovering how great it feels to be spiritually profitable every day. You want your family to get on this level with you, and that's great—but you've got to give them time. It's not fair to anyone to expect them to just jump to where you are.

And you have to expect that, for better or worse, they might not want to start living the way you're living now.

For family and friends

I want to include some thoughts here specifically for those of you reading this who are dealing with a family member or friend struggling with addiction.

Firstly—I get it.

I completely understand that your loved one's addiction has put you through hell. And at this point, you have every right to be skeptical. You've probably had your hopes built up before only to see things fall apart again. You've probably already heard your loved one at some point tell you that *this* time things are going to be different, really—only for them to slip right back into their old destructive patterns.

Maybe you're feeling burnt out. Maybe you're feeling bitter. Maybe you're feeling doubtful, resigned, frustrated, or one of a million other things.

I get it.

You have every right to be cautious and skeptical, but please do it with love and openness. Understand that your loved one is going through a lot of changes. If they stick with it and do what they need to do, they're going to be very different in a month. But also understand that, for better or worse, addiction and sobriety aren't like a light switch that's flipped either on or off. They're like a dimmer switch, slowly bringing up the lights. So yes, it's going to take time for your loved one to grow and change. But they are growing and changing.

You've got to be able to depend on yourself

Let's face it: you can't control how anyone in this world acts, except yourself. You are the only person that you're in charge of. No matter how much you might want to, you will never be able to control how another person sees you or acts around you. That's just not how life works.

You can control how you see yourself and how you live your own life. If you want to succeed in your sobriety, you have to know that at the end of the day, it's all up to you. That doesn't mean you won't have people on your team along the way, or that you'll be alone on this journey your whole life. There will of course be people around you offering support and camaraderie. It means that if your sobriety is going to be successful, it has to start and end with *you*.

As with so much else we've talked about, this applies everywhere in life too. If your commitments and your values are dependent on how other people act around you, you're rolling the dice and giving your power away. If you're only going to stay in shape if other people around you are staying in shape too, then it's probably only a matter of time before you quit going to the gym. If you're only going to eat healthy if everyone around you is constantly supporting you in it, then it probably won't be long until you're eating pizza for breakfast again.

How you live your life is up to you, and you alone. The good news is that when you embrace that truth, no one else can knock you off course. When you're the captain of your own ship, you steer the course—and no one can stop you from steering to the life that you want to live.

Chapter Twenty-Five
Conclusion

Just recently, I was driving back from Mammoth Lakes with my wife. We stopped at a gas station, and I ran in to grab a water and snack.

At the worst of my worst, I was living in Lake Tahoe, blowing through obscene amounts of cocaine. I've shared with you some of the stories from that time in my life, so you have an idea of just how off-the-rails and out-of-control my addicted life then was.

So here I am, driving through a place where the scenery isn't all that different. Feels a little familiar.

I'm in the gas station, and there's another guy in there who's buying a 40 oz bottle of Corona. Keep in mind, it's 8:30am, so this fella is not messing around. On top of that, he looks just like a guy I used to buy drugs from. I do a double take, standing there with my banana and bottle of water while this guy who could be my old drug dealer's twin buys his morning 40 oz.

Suddenly, I feel myself getting pulled back. My mind is traveling back to those days in Lake Tahoe, to all the thousands of dollars I spent buying drugs from that dealer. It's been over a decade since I've used, but I still feel the urges creeping in.

I couldn't help but laugh at the whole situation. Over a decade sober and this stuff still pops up from time to time. Like I've said, no matter how much weight you've lost or how healthy you might be eating now, a cheeseburger and ice cream are always going to sound tasty.

The urges still creep in sometimes, but now I'm able to just smile and laugh at them. Because now I know what to do.

So, I take a deep breath and start practicing the steps I've laid out for you in this book. I go back to the car, share the experience with my wife, we share a chuckle about it, and move on. Before too long, my head is on straight again.

This is the real deal—I know because I've lived it

Everything that is in this book is something I've lived and practiced. Every single concept, every exercise, every encouragement and warning. All of it comes directly from experience. I've been in a place that felt hopeless and broken beyond repair, but I pulled myself out, step by step, by practicing everything in this book.

And I still do.

These exercises and skills aren't something I ever 'finished' with. There's no magical finish line that addicts cross, where the personal development stops and addiction is no longer a factor in their lives. It's truly a lifelong journey.

I know sometimes that sounds discouraging. Human beings love quick and instant fixes. We want personal development to be something that we can buy at the corner drug store—hopefully on sale. We want that instant gratification of flipping a switch and moving on. But that's just not how life works, folks. Doesn't matter if you're an addict or not.

But I see now that this is a blessing.

My years of practicing everything I've laid out here hasn't just kept me away from relapsing back into addiction. It's had me grow as a person, and it's directly responsible for every wonderful part of the life I live now. I'm married to the girl of my dreams and I have a loving, connected relationship thanks to the work

I've done on myself. It's what has made it possible for me to have the friendships I have, the business success I enjoy, the beautiful home I live in. It's what has me wake up every morning excited for a new day, excited for what's ahead of me, excited to be alive.

This is what I want for you.

Not just for you to stay away from drugs or booze or whatever your old addiction was. Sure, that's part of it, but that's just the surface level. I want you to have a fulfilling, joyful, enriched life. I want you to be spiritually profitable at new levels every day, finding your rhythm in the world and living the life you've always wanted.

And everything I've laid out in this book is your path to get there.

If there's one final thought I could leave you with, it would be this: be humble. A healthy dose of humility is what makes everything here possible. My life finally took a turn when I was humble enough to admit that I wanted to change and that I needed help to make it happen.

Being humble had me listen to the wisdom of others—and their blunt feedback when I needed to hear it. Being humble made it possible for me to take a good long look at myself, including the rough patches, and start working on myself from the inside out.

When I look at the world today, I see a whole lot of problems caused by a lack of humility. In fact, I think just about every problem in the world boils down to a raging ego and lack of humility. War, famine, poverty, divorce, resentment, broken friendships. If we all chose to be humble, we could solve all of these problems.

I know that in the depths of addiction, it can sometimes feel like your problems are impossible to solve. But even if drug addiction or alcoholism or gambling addiction or any other addiction has completely taken over your life, you can fix it. The human soul can take an incredible amount of abuse and still bounce back, stronger than ever.

And I believe in you.

You can do this. I know you can, because I did. I know you can, because I've worked with countless addicts whose lives were in ruin, and I've seen them turn their lives around. I've seen them years later, happy, successful, and prosperous. That is possible for you—I promise.

All it takes is humility and a willingness to do the work, day in and day out. It's a long road, but it leads to a great life. You deserve that. And I'm on your team.

So, let's buckle up and get moving. I'll see you on the road.

Be Brave,

Ross Remien

About the Author

Ross is a Chemical Dependency Counselor and life coach with over 10 years of experience in the field of addiction. He opened Rebos Treatment Center in Los Angeles six years ago, which is now one of the most renowned outpatient treatment centers in the country.

Ross became involved in the treatment field after over 16 years of personal addiction to drugs and alcohol. After spending much of his life in the throes of active addiction, he felt compelled to challenge the stigma of addiction and became a leader in the advancement of recovery advocacy and treatment methods.

Ross currently lives in Los Angeles with his wife, Meg, and their two dogs, Arlo and Duke. They also live part-time in Mammoth Lakes, California, where he's an avid outdoorsman.